THE
Renegade
PASTOR'S GUIDE TO
MANAGING THE
STRESS
OF MINISTRY

Dr. Nelson Searcy & Richard Jarman

By Dr. Nelson Searcy and Richard Jarman
© 2019 Nelson Searcy
THE RENEGADE PASTOR'S GUIDE TO MANAGING THE STRESS OF MINISTRY

Published by Church Leader Insights U.S.A.

The graphic multicolored fan is a registered trademark of Church Leader Insights.
"Renegade Pastor" is a registered trademark of Nelson Searcy.

Library of Congress Cataloging-in-Publication Data
Searcy, Nelson
The Renegade Pastor's Guide to Managing the Stress of Ministry /
Nelson Searcy; with Richard Jarman
p. cm.
Includes bibliographical references.
ISBN: 978-0-9991523-1-7
Religion – Christian Ministry – Pastoral Resources

Unless otherwise indicated, Scripture quotations are from the Holy Bible,
Christian Standard Bible Translation, copyright © 2017 by Holman Bible Publishers.
Used by permission of Holman Bible Publishers. All rights reserved.

Scripture quotations labeled NLT are from the Holy
Bible, New Living Translation, copyright © 1996, 2004, 2015 by Tyndale
House Foundation. Used by permission of Tyndale House Publishers,
Inc., Carol Stream, Illinois 60188. All rights reserved.

The author has added italics to Scripture quotations for emphasis.

Printed in the United States of America
First Edition 2018

CONTENTS

INTRODUCTION

Pastor Alex Average leads a growing, busy congregation. He is occupied all the time with the cares of ministry. So many things stress him out: elder meetings, counseling church members, care for the church property, overseeing the weekend worship service planning, and sermon prep, just to name a few. Alex feels like he could be more effective as a minister of the gospel if he had a better handle on the stress of his vocation.

In addition, Alex has a loving family. His wife and kids are completely supportive of Alex's ministry. But they see the effects of stress in his life. He doesn't always have time for family activities, and when he does participate in family functions, sometimes he appears distant or frustrated. Ministry concerns intrude on family time, as much as he tries to avoid it. He doesn't exhibit the same joy for life or ministry that he once had. In particular, Alex's wife worries about the ways that the stress of being a pastor is affecting his life.

Pastor Alex also notices that his health is showing the effects of stress. He's gained a bit of weight over the years due to a poor diet fueled by stress eating. His blood pressure is higher than it ought to be. His doctor tells him he is prediabetic and faces a lifetime of insulin injections as a result. Alex knows that he needs to exercise, but he spends so much energy putting out ministry fires that pop up daily that he rarely finds the time.

Alex deeply loves being a pastor. And his congregation loves him. He is wise, kind, and compassionate. He is a fine leader and a powerful preacher. He sees God at work though his ministry. But he wonders how long he can continue as a pastor. The stress that he experiences is constant. It is relentless. It affects his family life. It is affecting his health. And it may be leading him toward an early grave.

• • • • •

Pastor Rob Renegade leads a growing congregation of people who look to him for vision, love, and wisdom as they fulfill God's mission for them in their city. Rob often tells people, "Pastoral ministry is not for the faint of heart!" It is tough. He faces all the same challenges that Alex, and every other pastor, does. Yet he appears to handle whatever comes his way. He doesn't show signs of being overly stressed; he isn't irritable with staff. He maintains a calm, peaceful demeanor that emanates from deep within his being.

Rob works long hours, but when he's home, his full attention is on his family. His wife and kids appreciate that he doesn't miss important family activities. He enjoys a regular date night with his wife — it's a highlight of his week. Perhaps most importantly, he is able to enjoy family time without being consumed by work stress, because he's learned to handle that stress.

Pastor Rob is in good health. He eats well, even with his busy schedule. He plans his meals as carefully as possible. He makes time for regular exercise. As a result, his doctor is very pleased with his overall physical health.

Rob looks to the future with a great deal of optimism. He knows that ministry will never get easier. It will always be tough. But he has built structures into his life and ministry that help him survive, and even thrive, when stressful times come.

Which pastor do you relate most to — Alex or Rob? Far too many pastors know what it's like to be Alex, drowning in the stress of pastoral ministry. In a Schaeffer Institute study of 1,050 pastors, every one of them said they knew a colleague or seminary friend who left the ministry due to stress.[1] We are losing a lot of good, godly men and women because they can't handle the pressures of being a pastor. How pervasive and destructive is stress in pastoral ministry? Well, in a recent survey of 4,400 Australian church leaders, a quarter of them said they were experiencing burnout as an extreme or significant issue. Half of the respondents said they were on the edge of burnout.[2] That's three quarters of pastors who see stress and burnout as a relevant issue in their personal ministries!

We don't want you to be an average pastor, fighting against the unstoppable tide of ministry stress. We want you to be like Rob Renegade, moving with a sense of peace and purpose, with many fruitful years of peaceful ministry. In fact, every day in my coaching networks, I (Nelson) see Renegade Pastors who are fighting the war against ministry stress — and winning!

THE EFFECT OF STRESS ON PASTORS

We probably don't need to convince any of you who are reading this book that pastoral ministry is demanding. Leading God's people is a pressure-packed occupation. You are the point person, the one everyone looks to for vision and leadership. You may lead a staff of pastors, or you may be the only paid staff member. In most cases, you are expected to lead in evangelistic outreach, discipleship training, and worship planning. You are often called upon to counsel church members in their crisis moment. Oh, and there's that minor issue of teaching Bible studies and preaching from God's Word!

As if that weren't enough, many of us have families whom God has entrusted us to lead. Spouses and kids demand, and deserve, our time and attention — not just our leftovers. The thought that our families may be missing out because of ministry pressures can make us feel like we are failing both God and our families (which, of course, adds to our stress).

Being a pastor is a spiritual endeavor, and we often let our physical bodies go. It's so easy to eat poorly and let exercise go by the wayside. As pastor Steve Reynolds, my (Nelson's) co-author for the book *The Healthy Renegade Pastor*, says, "Christians are the fattest people group on earth!" And unfortunately, pastors are the fattest, most out-of-shape Christians. Studies consistently show that pastors have rates of obesity, arthritis, depression, heart problems, high blood pressure, and diabetes that far exceed the national average.

Of course, stress doesn't take only a physical toll on pastors. Many pastors pay the price mentally, emotionally, and spiritually as well. They report that they are lonely, with few or no close friends they can confide in. Many pastors, rightly or wrongly, feel that they can't form close friendships with their church members. And they spend so much time working in their church that they don't have time or energy to invest in building relationships outside the church.

The emotional toll stress takes on us can be devastating. As we stated earlier, pastors often describe themselves as depressed. With depression comes a loss of energy and less joy in life. It also makes you more likely to make poor choices — choices you wouldn't make if not depressed. Everything from financial impropriety to moral failings can potentially be explained by the stress, isolation, and depression that pastors experience.

We are made to live in community, but with such busy schedules, it is difficult for pastors to develop outside activities or networks of friends. As a result, ministry can be a very lonely place. Pastors who are godly, intelligent, committed, driven, and called by God can suffer. In a recent Lifeway survey, 55 percent of pastors agreed that pastoral ministry made them feel lonely at times. Interestingly, the same survey found that 98 percent of pastors said it was a privilege to be a pastor.[3] So, pastoral ministry is both a privilege and a lonely, sometimes depressing, calling.

EXPERIENCING GOD'S BEST IN YOUR MINISTRY

Many would ask, "Is this what God intended for pastors? Are we meant to be isolated, depressed, alone, and stressed out by the demands of ministry?" We believe the answer is no.

That is not the kind of "average" ministry that God is calling you to. The fact that you are reading this book tells us that you want to be more than average. You want to go against the tide. You want to be a Renegade! And we are here to help you.

The truth is that ministry will always be hard. It will always be stressful. And, if you think about it, that makes sense. After all, is there a more important job in the world than being a local church pastor? The local church is God's vehicle for delivering the good news of salvation to the entire world. A job that big, a mission that immense, will naturally carry some stress with it.

The question is not, Will there be stress in ministry? The question is, How are you going to respond to the stress of ministry? In this book, we are going to give you specific strategies for handling stress in a way that makes your ministry lengthier and more fruitful.

As a Renegade Pastor, you approach ministry differently. You look for God's best, not settling for an average life. You realize that the stress of ministry is manageable — and you are determined to manage it!

When you apply the techniques you will learn in this book, you will see the benefits almost immediately. Effective stress management will mean a more fruitful ministry. So many pastors become firefighters, moving between crises and putting out fires in their ministry. They don't have the time or energy to dedicate to important tasks like sermon prep and vision casting. As a result, these activities suffer from lack of attention and are never fully developed.

When you can manage stress effectively, you are going to see an improvement in your family life. Imagine being fully present and engaged when you are watching your kid's soccer game or at dinner with your spouse. Imagine not having stress or nagging worries steal your attention and your joy. Your home life will be richer and fuller. Your spouse and kids will get the best of you, not just what you have left over after stress takes its toll on you.

God created our bodies as well as our spirits, and He doesn't want the effects of stress to ravage them. If you follow the advice we give in this book, you will find yourself in better physical shape than you are today! How can we say that? Because part of stress management involves taking care of ourselves physically. We are going to encourage you, and give you strategies, so that you exercise enough to keep stress at bay. We also give you strategies to help you avoid the bad eating habits that can creep up on you so quickly.

We were created for community. God didn't make us to live as Lone Ranger Christians. He wants us to have deep, satisfying friendships with others. He wants us to be able to share the joys and sorrows of ministry. We are going to give you strategies that will help you develop those kinds of friendships. When we share life together, we find ourselves stronger, more able to withstand the stress of a life of pastoral ministry.

With all these pieces in place, you will see the positive effects on your ministry. The first benefit you are likely to see is that you will be able to serve longer in vocational ministry. We see too many pastors who leave their calling, not because God calls them somewhere else, but because they just can't take it anymore. But we need good pastors. Pastors who will faithfully preach the gospel. Pastors who will lead God's people into the lives God intended for them to live. Pastors who will stand strong, no matter what. To be that kind of pastor for a lifetime of ministry, you must know how to manage stress.

Not only will your ministry be longer, it will be deeper. What do we mean by that? Depth in ministry comes when we are able to think and pray deeply about what God has for us and the churches we serve. Depth comes when we can study without distraction, because we aren't being torn apart by nerve-wracking situations. Depth comes when our church can depend on us to be the voice of God, leading them through sometimes uncertain waters. Depth comes when we are faithful and committed to God's purposes for our lives.

When you are able to manage stress well, you will see your ministry multiply in fruitfulness. Fruitfulness, in our definition, is simply doing what God has called you to do and doing it to the best of your ability. God may not call you to lead a megachurch. But He does call all of us to work with all we have in the field where He places us. Stress robs us of the energy we need. This book will help you handle stress better and enable you to put your full energy toward the things that matter most.

We also have a hope that this book will benefit not just you but also the next generation of pastors and church leaders. The truth is, none of us will be here forever. God will call us to His eternal reward someday. What kind of legacy are we leaving for the next generation — a legacy of frazzled, stressed-out leadership? Or a legacy of peace in the midst of storms? How we handle stress will largely determine the kind of legacy we leave behind.

More importantly, what will our kids remember about us? Will they remember that serving God was taxing, overwhelming, depressing? Or that their mom or dad served God faithfully and loved his or her family well? The choice is ours.

All of these are great reasons why you, as a Renegade Pastor, need this book on stress management.

PASTOR TO PASTOR

We are convinced that no one can understand the stress that comes with pastoral ministry quite like another pastor. After all, who knows better than another pastor what pastors go through? There are some things you can't know unless you experience it firsthand. No amount of reading, education, or training can prepare you for some of the things that happen to pastors on a daily basis. We know about the stress of pastoral ministry because we are pastors.

Meet Nelson Searcy

I am Nelson Searcy. I am the senior pastor of The Journey Church, which I founded in New York City in 2002. We currently have campuses in various New York City locations, as well as in Boca Raton, Florida, where I serve as pastor. We have been featured as one of the fastest-growing churches in the country. We have also been mentioned in articles in *Rolling Stone* magazine, as well as *The New York Times*. Throughout our history, we have met in different locations, including comedy clubs, movie theaters, and concert halls. We reach a diverse group of people in many different ways with the unchanging message of salvation through Jesus Christ.

I am also the founder of Church Leader Insights (CLI), an organization dedicated to helping local church leaders grow into the leaders God has called them to be. We have developed dozens of resources for pastors and church leaders, to help them "do Church" more effectively. I am probably best known for my work on the eight systems of a healthy church. Every church has eight main systems: assimilation, evangelism, stewardship, ministry, strategy, small groups, leadership, and worship planning. At CLI, we help pastors build healthy systems, which in turn leads to a healthy church.

Over the past decade, I have had the pleasure of coaching thousands of pastors from all over the country and around the world. In my coaching programs, I help dedicated pastors make the changes that maximize growth and health in their churches. As a coach, I hear the frustrations that so many pastors experience and help them develop strategies to alleviate that stress.

I have also written over fifteen books on topics ranging from church planting to assimilating guests to fostering generosity.

Through my books, I have been able to have an impact on the lives of thousands of pastors and church leaders.

I have had the privilege of being married to my best friend, Kelley, since 1994. She has been my constant companion in North Carolina, California, Manhattan, and Boca Raton, Florida. Along with our son, Alexander, we now call Boca home.

I've done denominational evangelistic work in North Carolina. I also headed up the Purpose Driven Network of churches, which has more than 5,000 member churches. I have degrees from Gardiner-Webb University and Duke University. I have also studied at Gardiner-Webb School of Divinity and Southern Baptist Theological Seminary.

Meet Richard Jarman

I am Richard Jarman. I am the senior pastor of TouchPoint Church in Bell Gardens, California, just outside Los Angeles. We are a growing, diverse congregation that has been in this urban area for the last eighty years. We are heavily engaged in our community, working especially with kids in the foster care system and with people recovering from drug and alcohol addiction.

I also teach church history and evangelism at the extension for Gateway Seminary, and I recently co-authored another book with Nelson, *The Renegade Pastor's Guide to Time Management* (also highly recommended!).

I have been married to my best friend, Jennifer, since 1999. We have five children(!), ranging in age from 16 to 8. We enjoy the many activities our kids are involved in, and we are also avid swing dancers. If I am not doing pastoral work or kids' events, Jennifer and I are probably dancing up a storm.

I have a bachelor's degree in history from California State University, Long Beach, and a master of divinity degree from Golden Gate Seminary (now Gateway Seminary).

HOW CAN THIS BOOK HELP YOU?

As you can see, both of us know from experience what kind of stress a pastor faces. Yet we have found strategies that help us so that we can maintain a healthy ministry and a balanced family life. We want to help you do the same.

After you read this book and apply what it says, you should notice some significant changes in your life:

- *A more fruitful pastoral ministry.* As we said before, stress robs you of energy. It makes you less willing to move and grow as God calls you to. When you manage your stress, you free up energy that you can channel into fruitful ministry.

- *Improved family time.* Just about every pastor wishes that he or she could spend more time with family. With your stress under control, that will be possible. And the time you spend with your spouse and kids will be better, because you won't spend that time worried about crises at church.

- *Greater level of health.* Stress makes us overeat and saps us of the energy we need to exercise. With a handle on your stress, you will be able to get the physical exercise you need. Your improved physical health will result in more energy and a brighter mood.

- *More time for friends and hobbies.* You must have other people in your life — people you can share with, people who can support you and whom you can support. Plus, we need to have activities we enjoy outside of ministry. When you manage stress well, you have time and energy for friends and hobbies.

HOW TO USE THIS BOOK

We have put this book together so that it is easy to use and implement quickly. (After all, we don't want reading this book to cause you extra stress.) So, we cover one strategy at a time — one concept that will help decrease your stress level or help you handle stress better.

We have designed this book so that each chapter stands alone, meaning that you don't need to read the chapters sequentially to get a benefit from the book. If there is a certain area you struggle with, read the chapter dealing with that issue first. Then work through the other chapters. Whatever order you read the chapters in, you will see the results.

Some of you have probably realized that I (Nelson) have an audio resource available from Church Leader Insights that deals with stress management. Although this book covers some of the same topics as that resource, this book goes into much more detail. In addition, much of the material is completely new and different. (To get the maximum benefit, I encourage you to check out my complete Stress Management Seminar, which you can download now for FREE at www.RenegadeStressManagement.com.)

Now it is time to get started. Before we begin, we want to ask you to do one thing: as you read, listen for the Holy Spirit as He speaks to you through this book. When we get down to it, stress management is a spiritual exercise. It is all about making the most of what God has given us, without the distractions caused by stress.

We know that as you read, the Holy Spirit will bring to mind some specific things that you need to do or that you need to stop doing. When those things come to mind, write them down. Don't ignore them. Don't depend on your memory, hoping to remember them later. Write them down, then act on what God has shown you as quickly as you can.

God wants you, as a Renegade Pastor, to be a fruitful, faithful minister of the gospel. He wants you, as a Renegade Pastor, to rise above average as you pursue God's best for you, your family, and your ministry. The next move is yours. Are you ready to go Renegade?

Chapter 1

KNOW THE DIFFERENCE BETWEEN GOOD AND BAD STRESS

You will keep the mind that is dependent on you
in perfect peace, for it is trusting in you.
Isaiah 26:3

When you ask Alex Average if he understands stress in ministry, he will emphatically answer, "Of course!" He finds nearly everything about being a pastor stressful. He has a particularly difficult elder board, with several members of that group speaking out against every initiative he comes up with. There are ongoing financial issues at church. The congregation looks to Pastor Alex Average for answers, but he finds answers hard to come by. These ongoing issues weigh heavily on him. He sometimes wonders how long he can stay in a position where the stress is relentless and unending.

Some pastoral activities cannot be avoided, and they occur on an ongoing basis. They cause stress for Alex. There's never enough time for sermon preparation. He wishes he could spend more time counseling his members. He would love to be able to do more to add joy to his life, but the demands of ministry appear to cut off that possibility.

Pastor Alex lives with the stress of ministry almost constantly. He feels some level of dread much of the time, even when he's enjoying time with his family. He finds that stress robs him of sleep on many nights. His energy level has dropped from what it once was. He is still a strong, energetic leader. But he is not as strong as he was — and he knows that stress is a big reason why.

Pastor Rob Renegade also knows stress. He has pastored his church for a number of years. It's a growing congregation, with all the good and bad that comes with growth. He is building the church with good systems in place, because he knows that if he goes through the work of establishing the systems properly, it will save him hassle later on.

Pastor Rob also knows that not all stress is the same. Some stress, like that which comes from building good systems in his church or even preparing his sermon, is short-term, and it comes with a reward once it's done. Other types of stress, such as counseling people in crisis or dealing with cranky elders, are ongoing and don't have easy resolutions. (Often, there is no solution at all in these situations.)

Pastor Rob has come to almost look forward to the kinds of "good stress" that he experiences. He knows that these activities, even though they may be difficult to undergo at the time, come with a reward that makes the stress worth it. He has actually begun to enjoy the good stresses in his life! At the same time, he is learning strategies that will help him deal with those other stresses — the ones that don't have an end date and that don't have any apparent resolution.

Through much trial and error, Rob has come to see some stress not as a curse, but as a gift from God. He tells people, "Sometimes God brings you through a dark valley so that he can give you a great blessing!"

NOT ALL STRESS IS THE SAME!

Pastor Rob Renegade has learned something very important: not all kinds of stress are the same. Some stress wears you down, decreases your joy, and separates you from those closest to you. Other kinds of stress can actually be energizing, show you that God is at work in your life, and bring you closer to friends and family. Let's take a look at these different kinds of stress. The key takeaway here: you want good stress in your life while you eliminate bad stress!

WHAT IS GOOD STRESS?

Psychologists identify some stress as good or beneficial. Often they refer to this type of stress as *eustress* (the prefix *eu* means "good"). Eustress, although it puts pressure on you and forces you to do difficult things, is actually good for you.

Most of us wouldn't accomplish much if we didn't have some level of stress in our lives. It's the pressure of deadlines, or the expectations of others, or the knowledge that we must get something done in order to receive a good reward, that motivates many of us to work toward certain goals. In reality, this kind of stress is a gift from God, pushing us to become what He has called us to be.

Good stress has certain characteristics that differentiate it from bad stress. One characteristic is that it gives you a burst of energy that can help you accomplish tasks quickly and efficiently. Anyone who has ever studied the night before an exam in school knows this feeling. Good stress gives you energy and focus.

Good stress can keep you out of dangerous circumstances. This might mean keeping you away from physical danger, like jumping out of the way of a moving car. Or it can steer you clear of emotional or organizational hazards. In the story on the previous page, Pastor Rob Renegade sees the danger of not having good systems in place, so he is going through some eustress to avoid potential disaster and the bad stress that would cause.

Some stress is actually good for your physical health. For example, you need to put some stress on your heart through vigorous cardio-vascular exercise in order to make it stronger. (Of course, consult your doctor before beginning an exercise program. You should also look at the chapter on exercise in my [Nelson's] book that I wrote with Steve Reynolds, *The Healthy Renegade Pastor*.)

In talking about this strategy, our goal is to help you see that you should never attempt to get rid of all stress in your life. In fact, nobody lives a life with no stress at all. As pastors, we will always have some level of stress. Our goal as pastors should be to minimize bad stress, while maximizing the benefits of good stress in our lives.

WHAT MAKES BAD STRESS BAD?

When most of us think of stress, we think of the harmful effects it has on us. To reduce this negative impact, we need to be able to recognize bad stress when it comes up. Here are some signs that the stress you are feeling is having a negative impact:

- *The source of the stress is ongoing, with no clear ending.* Since pastors deal with people all the time, and people can be difficult, this kind of stress hits pastors hard. In the story that began this chapter, Pastor Alex Average is locked in a difficult position with his elders. He must either find ways to resolve the conflict, or he will deal with the stress of the unresolved issue for the foreseeable future.

- *The stress is overwhelming.* While some stress is beneficial, too much stress is detrimental to your health. We see this in physical exercise. It's good to put your heart under some stress through cardiovascular exercise, but too much physical stress can cause a heart attack or stroke!

- *There is little reward attached to the stress, or the reward isn't readily apparent.* Pastor Alex Average's church has ongoing financial issues. If this pastor sees the opportunity here to teach his congregation about stewardship, this could be good stress that leads to greater faithfulness in the church. But if he doesn't act, this will continue to weigh on him.

- *The stress takes your energy and steals your joy.* When you have issues that aren't easily resolved, and when you see no end in sight, it's hard to find joy. We have all seen situations where someone is going through a chronic illness. Often people in this circumstance find it difficult to face the day, because the stress of their illness has taken their energy away.

Bad stress tears us down. It is destructive. Eventually, it will destroy our hope, our energy, our joy — even our ministry. But we can see that we need good stress to get things done. In this next section, we want to help you see good stress for what it is: a gift from God to help you grow and expand your ministry.

WHY GOD GAVE US GOOD STRESS

Stress is a gift from God! Does that sound like an odd statement, especially in a book that is committed to helping you manage stress? We will admit, it seems a little strange for us to make the statement. But we are both convinced that once we see that some kinds of stress are actually a blessing, it will transform the way we manage all our stress.

How is stress a gift? First, stress is a great motivator — if we allow it to be. The most precious resource any of us have is time. You have twenty-four hours in a day, no matter who you are. You can't buy more time or make more. Stress reminds us that certain things need to be done, and done in a timely manner.

It is so easy for us to get caught up in the busyness of ministry and forget about the value of time. (Please see our previous book, *The Renegade Pastor's Guide to Time Management*, for more about using time wisely.) We forget that we have just a short time here on earth to accomplish God's mission for our lives. So God uses stress as a prod to move us in the direction He wants us to go.

Another reason why stress can be a gift from God is that it helps us focus on what's most important in our lives. Stress is a form of pain, and pain is God's early-warning system, letting us know that something isn't right. For example, I (Richard) recently lost over 100 pounds and got in much better physical shape. My motivation for this lifestyle change was the pain and stress caused by being un-healthy. I got an infection that I couldn't shake because my body was in such bad shape. That motivated me to focus on an area of my life that I had neglected. Without that pain, I probably wouldn't have focused on my physical health, and it would have continued to deteriorate.

The larger lesson you can glean from that story is this: *Almost any stress can be good stress if you approach it the right way.* For example, the financial troubles that Alex Average's church consistently experiences are definitely a source of stress. If Pastor Alex chooses to address the problem directly and lead his people to greater faithfulness in their stewardship, then this will be good stress. It will be good because the pain that the pastor feels moved him to make changes that led to his congregation's growth.

Think of how energizing this concern could be for our pastor. He could plan a sermon series talking about the fact that generosity is a command from God, not just for the rich, but for every child of God. He might encourage his treasurer or financial board to make giving easier by implementing online giving and making sure giv-ing envelopes are readily available at every service. The result of this pastor's leadership would not only be better finances, it would be a re-energizing of his leadership. He would personally enjoy greater peace of mind, more confidence, and a confirmation of his abilities and calling as a pastor.

On the other hand, if Pastor Alex Average chooses to accept that financial troubles are just "the way things are," then this will be a source of negative stress. It will be an ongoing condition, with little prospect of it getting better on its own. It will weigh Pastor Alex down. Thoughts of the church's financial difficulties will quite possibly haunt our pastor, even when he's enjoying time with his family. In the most extreme scenario, it may even be one of the factors that drives this pastor from the ministry.

A REAL-LIFE EXAMPLE OF GOOD STRESS

When I (Richard) first came to the church I currently pastor, TouchPoint Church, the church was in bad shape in many ways. The weekly attendance was around 12. I knew the finances of the church were a mess. But I didn't know how big a mess they were until a couple of months after I accepted the call to pastor the church, when the property taxes came due.

I didn't realize that, for years, the church hadn't had the resources to pay the property taxes on time. We paid them, eventually, but often months late. That meant we paid heavy penalties in addition to our taxes. As I looked into it, I saw that we had nothing in our bank accounts with which to pay the taxes we owed. Knowing that we had several thousand dollars due in a matter of weeks, and no way to pay it, was very overwhelming. But I took action.

I focused my attention on teaching about stewardship. I taught, as Nelson encourages pastors to do in his Stewardship Seminar, that stewardship was part of discipleship. (To learn more about The Stewardship Seminar, go to www.RenegadeStressManagement.com.) Growing Christians give! I was honest with our little congregation about our needs. The result? Our people gave generously. We ended up having the money to pay the taxes. That was the beginning of getting our church healthy financially.

God used that stressor to help me grow. I got over my distaste about talking about money. I got much better at asking for people to give, without being manipulative. The whole ordeal bonded my heart to the people who were here, because we had been through something traumatic together. My faith grew and was strengthened because of it. I am a better pastor because of the stress and my response to it!

One of the other stress points mentioned in the story is the ongoing conflict Pastor Average has with his elder board. We are sure most pastors reading this have been in a similar situation: some leaders in the church are reluctant (to put it mildly) to follow the vision God has given you for the church. This can be a constant source of stress and frustration. In fact, we both know more than one pastor who has left a position in a church due to leadership that is just stuck in its ways.

Even a problem that looks as unsolvable as this can be seen as a source of good stress if the Renegade Pastor approaches the situation with the right attitude. For example, maybe the solution is as simple as opening more dialogue with the reluctant parties to find out what their concerns are. Perhaps you will need to work on your skills when it comes to having difficult conversations (which nobody really likes). Perhaps you will find that it's time to raise up new leadership and ask the old guard to step aside.

All of these are positive ways to handle this admittedly stressful situation. Although we certainly can't guarantee that the outcome will be positive, we can guarantee that if you approach it with the proper attitude, you can make good use of bad situations.

THE WAY GOD WORKS

You *can* see something good come out of stressful situations. We don't want to come across as preachers here (even though we are). But it might be helpful to remind ourselves that God is in the business of bringing good out of even the worst episodes imaginable. The Bible is full of stories of God's people being put in impossible situations.

From Joseph, to Moses, to David, to Paul and Jesus Himself, God can make good come out of bad circumstances.

We need to remember this fact when we face tough scenarios: nothing is beyond God's ability to redeem and heal. He brings together people who have been at odds for years. He provides financial solutions, sometimes in miraculous ways. We need to correctly identify stressful situations and plan a course of action to alleviate the stress. But we should never forget that God is also at work, bringing good out of challenging circumstances.

We hope that something else has become apparent as you have been reading this chapter: many of the stresses you will encounter in your ministry can be viewed as either good or bad. It all depends on the way you approach them. If you think something is hopeless or unwinnable, you often will make it so. If you believe there is a way out of the stress, and that God wants to teach you and your congregation through the ordeal, you will make that happen also. We are all really good at self-fulfilling prophecies.

HOW TO MAKE THE MOST OF GOOD STRESS

Good stress is good only if you get something out of it. Otherwise, even good stress can turn into a negative stressor. In this section, we will look briefly at what we can do to make the most of those circumstances where God may be using stress to help us, and our congregation, grow. Here are three great strategies to help you maximize the benefits of good stress:

- *See the opportunity that lies within the stressor.* If you are looking for it, there is an opportunity for growth and change in almost every stressful situation. In the case of my (Richard's) health transformation, the stress was my deteriorating health. But the opportunity was there for me to get healthier. I saw the opportunity and made the lifestyle changes that I needed to make.

The truth is that most stressors carry within them the seeds of growth. But if you aren't looking for those possibilities, you will definitely miss them. For a pastor, this provides a great opportunity for you to model the way you want your congregation to respond to stress. Choose to respond with hope, looking toward the opportunity for growth.

- *Never lose hope!* That brings us to the next key strategy for maximizing good stressors. It is our conviction that most people, including pastors, give up too easily. But you are not most people. As a Renegade Pastor, you know that it is always too early to give up. Even situations that look hopeless can change and be made better.

That doesn't mean we should always keep the same approach to a difficult situation. We may need a fresh assessment, or a different viewpoint on what to do. (That's one reason why it's often good to have someone else look at our situation: we can gain their perspective and insight.) But as long as we are alive, we should never lose hope.

- *Take action!* One thing we know for certain: if you don't do anything, nothing will change. Yes, we believe that God works miracles. We know He is capable of acting on His own, without our help. But normally, God works in response to our actions. The way it usually works is this: we move out in faith, take action, and then God works — often in ways we could never expect.

When we take action on a stressful situation, we are not showing a lack of faith. Rather, we are showing our faith in the God who works miracles. After all, the only reason to act is because we believe in God's power to change things!

When you do these things, you will find that many of the negative stressors in your ministry will operate as good stress. Or at the very least, you will find that there are aspects of those negative stressors that God can use to help you grow. Although those aspects might be painful at the time, they are designed by God to help you become the person He called you to be!

PUTTING THIS STRATEGY TO USE

It is vital that we remember not all stress is bad. If we fail to recognize this, we will likely find that stress is overwhelming. When we do maintain this perspective, we can learn to compartmentalize our stressors and adopt strategies that help us manage each one. Of course, you treat good stressors differently than you would negative stressors. (We will look at effective strategies for dealing with negative stressors in the following chapters.)

A proper perspective helps us face stressors with the right mindset. It also helps us face ministry stressors with faith. When we face problems that stress us out we often lose sight of God's bigger picture. He uses every circumstance in our lives, even the negative ones, to help us grow. If we don't approach these stressors with faith in God and His control over our lives, we are likely to miss what God has in store for us.

When you approach ministry stressors with faith, you are also maintaining hope that God will work to bless you, even in discouraging conditions. As a believer, and especially as a Renegade Pastor, you know that it is always too early to give up hope!

Keep in mind also that one thing that makes bad stress so bad is that it is ongoing, with no real end date. It has a tendency to wear you down. To get a benefit from this type of stress, it's important for you to set some end dates — at least for certain aspects of the stressful issue. For example, if you need to have a difficult conversation with an elder, schedule that meeting. When you set an end date, you can focus and maximize your productivity on the activity at hand.

Also, don't forget that God's plan for you is to grow you so you are more like Jesus. And growth is not always pleasant or easy. Growth is often a winding road — with some dead ends. When stresses come up in ministry, always ask yourself, "Is God trying to grow me through this stressful situation?"

When you change your perspective to look for opportunities for growth, you may see something that you would otherwise miss. Don't miss out on something that God has for you because you were looking only at the stress. God may have something bigger for you!

Stress has a tendency to paralyze us with fear. It tends to overwhelm us because it can look like it's about to take over every aspect of our lives. Instead, we should let stress be a motivator, something that moves us to action. Nothing about the stressful condition will change if we do not act. Of course we expect God to move — even to work miracles on our behalf. But God acts most often in response to, and in concert with, our activities. So trust God, and act knowing that God will work all things out for our good.

Lastly, consider what we said at the beginning of this chapter: not all stress is bad. Often, the difference between bad stress and good stress is simply your perspective. Always remember that for God, nothing is impossible. And nothing is beyond His ability to redeem. Continue to trust Him and His desire to use everything that happens to help us grow. Take action, and trust Him to use those good stressors to grow you and your ministry!

Learn to discern the differences between good stress and bad stress, and discover how stress can actually deliver benefits when you approach it with the right perspective. Before long, you will find it easier to handle those challenging conditions!

Chapter 2

GET CLEAR ABOUT THE SOURCES OF YOUR STRESS

Don't worry about anything; instead, pray about everything.
Tell God what you need and thank him for all he has done.
PHILIPPIANS 4:6

One of the things Alex Average finds most frustrating about being a pastor is also something that he finds somewhat exhilarating: he doesn't know where the next exciting/stressful moment is going to come from. There is always something happening. And he is a born problem-solver. He is a truly great leader, especially in times of crisis. It's during those really challenging times that Pastor Alex is able to shine.

But if he is going to be honest, the rush he gets from dealing with the various crises of ministry is usually overwhelmed by the constant stress and pressure. One of the things he finds most draining is the unpredictable nature of ministry stressors. He doesn't always even know where the stress is coming from, or what is causing him such discomfort. But he is clear on one thing: each time a new episode arises, it takes a little bit out of him. And Pastor Alex isn't sure how much more of it he can take.

Pastor Rob Renegade can't honestly say that he enjoys the demanding situations that pop up constantly in ministry. But he can say that he has become better at dealing with these circumstances. He knows that ministry will never be easy or stress-free. Rather than working toward a stress-free life, he has made it his goal to manage stress well so that he can be an effective minister of the gospel. Of course, he wouldn't say that he always handles stress well. But in most cases, he is able to keep ministry stress at a manageable level.

One lesson Pastor Rob has learned is that to manage stress, you must be clear about what is actually agitating you. That means you need to take the time to analyze stressful conditions and see which parts you find taxing. By analyzing challenging situations, Pastor Rob is sometimes able to break big problems into manageable parts. What he inevitably finds is that in every crisis situation, there are usually two or three things that he finds worrying or that he doesn't want to do. Then there are other things that either aren't so bad, or that he can delegate to someone else.

By becoming clear about what stresses him out, Pastor Rob is able to better deal with pressures. This makes him a more effective leader of his congregation. He looks forward to the future, knowing that he can have a long, fruitful ministry.

When I (Richard) was a kid growing up in southern California, we didn't have many thunderstorms. (After all, it's always sunny in Los Angeles!) But when we did have a thunderstorm, we would try to find out how close the storm clouds were to us. The way we would figure out the closeness of the storm was this: when we saw lightning, we would count the seconds between the lightning and the time we heard the thunder. The number of seconds between the lightning and the thunder was the number of miles away the storm was.

Now I have no idea if that is scientifically accurate. (My guess is that it's not accurate at all.) And, of course, this game wouldn't tell us *where* the storm was — only how far away it was.

But it was a fun game to play, and it kept our minds occupied so we weren't as afraid of the storm.

Finding clarity about where the stress of ministry is coming from is more than a game. It is a vital component of managing ministry stress. When you can discern the source of the pressure, often you will see a pathway that you can take to resolve problem situations. Other times, you will see that there are really only one or two aspects of a scenario that you find challenging, while other facets are merely minor annoyances. This is especially true when major crises hit.

When a big ministry crisis happens, often we get overwhelmed by the magnitude of it. That feeling of being overwhelmed can cause a kind of paralysis in our decision-making. It can cause an unhealthy fear, which keeps us from acting boldly. When we are able to be clear about which parts of a situation are causing us stress, not only is our stress level lowered, but our fear level will be as well. With our fear and stress under control, it is easier to make good decisions.

Finding clarity in the midst of a crisis is not an easy task. But it's vital that we do it. The first step in finding clarity is simply taking a step back to analyze the situation. You may not think you have time to look closely at the circumstances, but we would encourage you to do it anyway. The time you spend analyzing often saves you much more time later, as you can work on the problem much more effectively.

When assessing a stressful situation, do your best to be objective. This is often difficult, especially when there is conflict or emotions involved. You may want to ask the opinion of someone outside the situation, someone you can trust to give you an honest evaluation of what they see going on. (We all need good, godly people in our lives to give us support and counsel. We will take more time to discuss this in another chapter of this book.)

Sit down for a moment. Breathe. Pray. Break down the issue piece by piece. Once you have done that, you can focus on tackling the most pressing aspects first. (We also cover this — the idea that you need to do the most important thing first — in another chapter of this book.) Some of these tasks will, in fact, be daunting. You may need to have a difficult conversation with a reluctant elder. You may need to cut a long-standing program. But you will also find that other items that need to be handled aren't really that bad. They may not be your favorite activities, but they don't cause much stress at all.

We have seen this scenario play out repeatedly in our own ministries and the ministries of others: you begin to tackle some of the stressful items on your to-do list, and something amazing happens. Momentum kicks in! The next thing you know, you are making real progress. Your energy level increases, and you feel like doing even more. You gain focus and clarity. Before you know it, the once-overwhelming task is completed!

Of course, the opposite can also happen if you fail to take that initial step of figuring out exactly what is challenging in a given context. The task remains overwhelming. A sense of hopelessness or dread settles in. And it doesn't just affect that particular episode: soon that dread is creeping into other aspects of your ministry. You may even find yourself taking that dread home, infecting your family life. It drains you of focus and energy, making the process of resolving the difficult situation that much harder.

That's why it is so important to take the initial step of getting clarity about what is really going on. We said it before, but it's so important that we need to repeat it: *the time you spend finding out what is really going on and identifying the stressors you face is time well spent.* Don't allow the desire to "do something" make you take less effective action. Take time at the beginning to do an honest analysis. You save time when you are able to take effective, decisive action on the challenging issues you face.

DECEPTIVE STRESSORS

The reason why we need to take time to become clear about the real stressors we face is that often those stressors aren't readily apparent. They may even deceive us at first. This happens for a number of reasons:

- *Sometimes we are too close to a situation to make a good judgement about what's really happening.* We have all been there: we are in a conflict with another person, or someone has done something that irritates or offends us. Those things cause an immediate, natural emotional reaction in us. Under those conditions, it is often difficult to clearly see what's happening and how we should respond.

  This is a time when it is especially important to rely on the wisdom of others. When you are in an emotional situation, or when you have a lot invested in something, get someone you trust to be your eyes and ears. That may keep you from making decisions you later regret.

- *There may be underlying stressors you aren't consciously aware of.* We all have activities that make us angry, or nervous, or afraid. We find these things taxing. We may not even realize what those triggers are. We may not see that those are the tasks that are causing us great stress. When we take time to reflect, we may find that there is something particular that is causing the bulk of our stress.

  Many people, pastors included, have trouble with procrastination. When we put responsibilities off, it causes stress. But it may be just one thing that you find daunting, and that's the thing you need to address. For example, maybe you've been putting off following up with recent guests to your church. You need to write thank-you notes to some, send emails to others, and call a few more. But maybe you really dislike calling people, and that's what is derailing your progress. Once you realize that, you can come up with a strategy for dealing with this one thing you find stressful. (We recommend calling people right away to get it over with, but there are other effective strategies as well.)

- *Maybe you're not in a good place physically to do what needs to be done.* Fatigue is often the enemy of faith! If you are tired, you might find certain things overwhelming when they don't need to be. I (Richard) once had a mentor who told me, "Sometimes the most godly thing you can do is take a nap!"

We pastors like to think we are Superman, able to power our way through anything. But Renegade Pastors know that they are only human. Sometimes we just need to rest so we can have the strength to handle ministry stress another day. (We talk about the importance of physical well-being in handling stress in another chapter of this book.)

COMMON SOURCES OF STRESS

Of course, every church is different. Every pastor is wired differently, created distinctly by God to do something unique in His kingdom. Still, some things are common sources of stress to most, if not all, pastors:

- *The fact that the work is never done.* There is almost never a time when you can look at your desk and say, "There's nothing left for me to do!" As pastors, there is always unfinished business. That's just a part of the job that can't be helped.

Some personality types find it difficult to leave tasks unfinished. If you have one of those personality types, you will experience greater stress in ministry.

- *People. Just people.* Let's face it: people can be exhausting! We love them, but they can be draining. There is a never-ending string of problems, sin, and drama. And some people are especially taxing. They are emotional vampires, robbing you of time and energy.

  One of the toughest things about dealing with people is that you don't see the results of your ministry right away. Sometimes people struggle with sinful and destructive habits for years before they "get it" and change. Waiting for people to change can be difficult at best, as you wonder if the change will ever come.

- *Lone Ranger ministry.* We talk about this at more length in another chapter, but we will touch on it here. We are not meant to do ministry alone! That is *not* how God intended it to be. We need supportive people who can help us carry the weight of ministry.

  These supportive people don't need to be paid staff. They can be churchgoers who love you and want to serve God by serving you. Train others to take some of the burden off you. Not only will you find your burden lighter, but you will help other people find places where they can serve.

- *Repeated tasks.* Closely related to the idea that you never get completely finished with tasks is that some tasks are repeated over and over again, with no end. Probably the most obvious of these tasks is preaching, which requires an enormous amount of work every week. Many pastors find holidays, especially Christmas, to be stress-inducing.

  While you probably can't escape the stress of sermon preparation completely, you can find ways to make sermon planning less stressful. I (Nelson) have a resource on planning a one-year preaching calendar. For a free copy of this resource, visit www.RenegadeStressManagement.com. You can also check out my available resources on maximizing holidays and other big days at the same site. Use them to minimize your stress.

While none of these stressors can be eliminated completely, they can be identified. Once they are identified, you can develop strategies that will help you deal with them — and get them under control.

But the truth is, there are some stressors that we can't control. Quite a few, actually. So we need to look at what we can do to manage stress when we can't control those things that are causing the stress.

THE BIGGEST STRESSOR OF ALL?

We saved another common stressor for last. It may be the biggest, most challenging thing we face, and we are sure that nearly everyone has experienced this at some point. The stressor we are talking about here is the desire to control things that are out of our control. Too often, we find ourselves attempting to corral horses that don't belong to us! And God does not intend for us to live under this level of stress.

In the Bible, God tells us that there are certain things that we don't control. In Romans 12:18, it says, "If possible, *as far as it depends on you*, live at peace with everyone." That tells us pretty clearly that some things depend on us — and some things do not! We need to concentrate our efforts on the areas where we can make a difference.

If we are going to manage our stress well, we will need to recognize that we add to our stress levels by taking on responsibilities we can't possibly bear. What are some things we can't control? Here are a few:

- *The actions of other people.* People are unpredictable, at best. Even people we know well can do things that anger us, disappoint us, frustrate us. Now, we should do our best to surround ourselves with stable people, people on whom we can depend. But we need to expect that, on occasion, even the most dependable people will let us down.

- *Other people's reactions to you.* This will shock many of you, but some people are not going to like you! No matter what you do, no matter how hard you try to be pleasant or make connections with them. We should try to be "harmless as doves," as Jesus said. But you can't control how people react to you, especially when you put your best foot forward.

- *Facility limitations.* This is especially true if your church is in an established location. Your seating capacity is what it is. Your parking lot can hold a certain number of cars. No amount of stress or worry can change those facts. The best you can do is plan to minimize the effects of the limitations you have.

  Or, you can make plans to rebuild, remodel, or move your facilities. Each of those is certainly a possibility, and God may lead you in one of those directions. Until that happens, accept your limitations and plan accordingly.

- *Other limitations — in funds, volunteers, or anything else.* We know that, as a Renegade Pastor, you are committed both to personal growth and growth in your church. That will mean an expanding pool of resources. But at any given moment, you have a certain number of people, finances, or any number of things you need. Plan in faith, expect God to bless, and don't let present limitations stress you out.

- *Political changes.* Several years ago, when I (Richard) was at another church, the city we were in decided they would make it illegal for churches to be located in residential-zoned neighborhoods. The church I was at was located in the middle of a residential neighborhood! We were faced with the likelihood of having to move a church that had been there for seventy-plus years.

Fortunately, the city council came to its senses and decided not to pass such a regulation. But if they had, we would have had no say in the matter. Politics and politicians change all the time. You can seek to be a good influence, but you will be sorry if you allow the changing tides of politics to become a source of stress for you.

None of the things we listed are really under your control. Or they are things that can't be easily changed. Yet, many of us spend a lot of energy stressing about these things. That energy can be put to better use tackling issues that you can actually do something about.

It can be discouraging to realize that there are so many things that we don't control. Are we merely victims of circumstance? Should we just sit and wait for the next crisis to hit? Are we left to simply hope everything turns out okay? As a Renegade Pastor, the answer to these questions is a resounding NO! While we can't control everything around us, there is something we can control, no matter what happens.

CONTROLLING YOUR RESPONSE TO STRESS

When those inevitable stressors come, we can — *and must* — control how we respond to them. Often, our responses are more important than the actual conditions we are responding to. We have the power to make things better or worse, depending on how we respond.

Our responses are critical. The people around us will naturally emulate what they see us doing. Thus, our response is magnified and multiplied throughout our congregation. A good reaction will encourage your church to respond to crises with hope and faith. A negative response can do just the opposite.

The problem is that stressful situations don't often call to schedule an appointment. Instead, they drop in unannounced and unwanted — usually at the worst possible times. We need to decide beforehand how we are going to respond to difficult times. We suggest you make these four choices before the storm hits, so you will be ready when it does:

- *Choose hope over despair.* Even when it looks like there's no way out, you must rest in the fact that God is always in control. Since He is in charge, it is always too early to give up hope. We serve a living, powerful God!

- *Choose faith over fear.* It is natural to become afraid when we are faced with crises. But trust that God has a plan, even for this hard time. Trust Him to work something good out of very difficult circumstances. He can do great things in us and through us if we simply trust Him.

- *Choose peace over turmoil.* When we say this, we don't mean you should just try to achieve peace at all costs. Some things are worth fighting for. We believe that, as shepherds, we need to protect the sheep. Sometimes that takes a warrior's mentality. But we can go to war with the peace of Christ ruling in our hearts (Col. 3:15).

- *Choose action over inaction.* Stressful situations can paralyze us. What if we make the wrong move? What if there's more to the incident than we know? These are legitimate concerns. But inaction is almost always the wrong response. I (Nelson) often tell my coaching network partners to "run toward the conflict." Don't shy away from a predicament just because it's difficult.

Two things are almost always true. First, very few crises will resolve themselves without any action on your part. Something caused the stressor to happen, and something will need to be done to resolve it. Second, few mistakes are fatal. It's easier to recover from a misstep than it is to repair the damage done by doing nothing. Take bold action, walking in peace, hope, and faith.

WHAT IF I DON'T RESPOND CORRECTLY AT FIRST?

Let's face it: none of us are always going to respond correctly, especially when a challenging situation first hits. So let's talk briefly about what to do when we've had time to reflect and realize that we could have done things better. Here are three ideas about what to do if you find you've started handling a difficulty in an ineffective way:

- *Don't compound the mistake by continuing it.* It takes some courage to admit you've made a mistake. Sometimes it's easier to just keep plowing ahead, even if you're going the wrong direction. Stop! Repeating a mistake is much worse than making one in the first place.

- *Admit your error.* Most of us find it hard to admit to mistakes. But good leaders can say, "I blew it" and move on. Admitting your mistakes makes you a stronger, more transparent leader. And it gives those around you permission to make mistakes also.

- *Chart a new course.* You may have started down the wrong road. But you can always change the path you're on. The sooner you get started in the right direction, the sooner you can get to where you need to be.

There is not only one correct way to respond to any given difficult situation. With experience, and dependence on the Holy Spirit, we can hopefully achieve some level of clarity about the source of our stress. That, in turn, helps us chart a course of action that can resolve the challenging circumstance.

As you seek clarity about the stressors in your life, keep these things in mind:

- *It's always a good idea to take a moment and look at a difficult issue.* The time you spend in reflection will save you time by helping you focus your attention on taking effective action.

- *In your reflection time, you can identify the items that you are finding especially challenging in any given situation.* It's usually a good idea to tackle these "big stressors" first in order to build momentum that will help you accomplish more.

- *Don't be afraid to get a second pair of eyes looking at the scenario.* Often, someone who isn't as close to the situation can see more clearly just what is going on. They can help you get the clarity you desperately need.

- *There are some things you just can't control, and you shouldn't waste time and energy stressing out about them.* Learn to make the most of your current limitations, even while working to enlarge the scope of your ministry.

- *Although you can't control everything that happens, you DO have control over your response to what happens.* We encourage you to make four choices:

  o   Choose hope over despair.
  o   Choose faith over fear.
  o   Choose peace over turmoil.
  o   Choose action over inaction.

When you choose to respond this way, you are already ahead of the game!

- *When you do respond incorrectly in a stressful circumstance, remember that few mistakes are fatal.* Don't compound your mistake by continuing it. Instead, admit your mistakes, apologize for your errors, and move forward in the correct direction.

When you follow these guidelines, you will find that you can handle stressful situations more easily. And, like any habit, the more you do it, the easier it becomes. Get better at identifying the sources of your stress, and act to resolve them whenever possible.

Chapter 3

MANAGE YOUR TIME WELL

Teach us to number our days carefully, so that we may
develop wisdom in our hearts.
PSALM 90:12

Alex Average knows that it is a calling from God to lead His people. But he often wonders why this calling has to be so difficult. Alex feels like he is constantly behind schedule. That is, if he has a schedule. He tries to keep a regular calendar, but he finds it frustrating. Unexpected events, longer-than-anticipated wait times, and traffic eat away at his time. Being late all the time really bothers him.

Not only is he chronically late, he often forgets things. Last week, he missed a lunch meeting with another pastor. He felt like he needed that time of fellowship and encouragement. But he had to go without because he simply forgot. Pastor Alex's perpetual lateness and occasional forgetfulness leaves people with the false impression that he isn't very professional. He wishes he had more time for his family, and more time to prepare his sermons each week. But there just doesn't seem to be enough hours in the day for him to get everything done.

When it comes to being busy, Pastor Rob Renegade knows all about it. He manages to keep his time under control, however. He has learned techniques that help him get the most out of every day. His calendar is full, but it's manageable. He sees that good time management is critical if he is going to accomplish everything God has for Him to do.

Pastor Rob is rarely late for appointments. If he says he will be somewhere, you can be assured that he will be there. He gets a lot done — more than most people. He doesn't waste time waiting in line when it isn't necessary. He plans extra commuting time if he must drive during high-traffic times. Because he is consistent in these practices, he is usually a few minutes early to appointments.

His promptness and reliability give him a reputation as someone who can be depended upon. His family appreciates that they know he will be present at family functions. Pastor Rob invests a few minutes each day in planning his next day's calendar — and that investment comes back to him in the form of hours saved every week!

WE WROTE THE BOOK ON TIME MANAGEMENT

How important is time management to us? We wrote an entire book on time management for Renegade Pastors. (Learn more at Amazon.com.) The truth is, if you can manage your time well, you will be better able to handle stress. Our time management book goes into great detail about how to manage this critical area. In this chapter, we just want to give you a few tips that will help you manage your time, and therefore your stress, more wisely.

YOUR MOST PRECIOUS RESOURCE

Time is the most important resource that God gives us. It is the only resource you can't make more of. Think about it: once the twenty-four hours we call "today" is gone, it's gone forever. Nothing you can do will bring it back.

With that being true, it becomes easy to see that every minute is precious. We firmly believe that it is a sin to waste time. After all, wasting time is, in essence, telling God, "I don't want this precious gift you're giving me — the gift of this moment."

As human beings, we are bound by time. Everything we do has time restrictions. One of the things that many pastors find daunting is the need to fit everything we have to do into our schedules. That is a difficult — sometimes impossible — task. In this chapter, our aim is to give you a few next-level time-saving and stress-relieving tips.

TIME-SAVING TIP #1: DON'T START THE DAY UNTIL YOU PLAN THE DAY

We have heard pastors say something like, "I don't keep a calendar. I let the Holy Spirit plan my day." Now that may sound very spiritual, but we believe it is a terrible idea for Renegade Pastors. Although it's true that not everything goes according to plan, you need to start with a plan. Take time, preferably the night before, to plan what your next day is going to look like.

If you don't plan your day ahead of time, you will find yourself at the mercy of other people's ideas of how your day should go. And their ideas probably won't line up with yours! Here are some practical ideas on how to plan your day:

- *Plan according to your priorities.* Know what's important to you, and make sure you spend time every day working in those areas. When you work in areas that are a priority for you, it naturally increases your focus and energy, and lowers your stress level. The opposite is also true: If you spend too much time working on things that aren't important to you, you lose focus and energy — and you gain stress!

- *Plan your devotional time.* If it doesn't go on your calendar, it probably won't happen. So build time in your schedule for your time alone with God in prayer and Bible study. Then guard this time jealously — the devil will try to make you too busy to spend time with God. Many people have a rule of "No Bible, no breakfast," meaning that their morning devotional time comes first, even before eating. That's a good way to get your day started off right.

- *Be realistic about the amount of time activities take.* We both live in areas notorious for high-traffic conditions — South Florida (Nelson) and Southern California (Richard). Traffic is just a fact of life, and we must always factor it into our driving time. On the other hand, many pastors are unrealistic about how long it takes to do tasks like sermon preparation and filing paperwork. We need to get an accurate assessment of the time it takes to get things done. Figure out how long it takes to do certain tasks, and factor that time into your schedule.

- *Plan family time.* Again, if it isn't on your calendar, it likely won't happen. So be sure to remember your family. Your most important ministry is to your spouse and children. Don't give them your leftover time. Put family activities on the calendar, and don't let anything take their place. Vital: Put a date night with your spouse on the calendar *every week.* You need this to keep your marriage strong and growing.

- *Plan blocks of "alone time."* Average pastors have an open-door policy, where people are invited to drop in on them at any time. Renegade Pastors plan times when they are not available to anyone. They use this time to plan, pray, reflect, and write. These are activities that need your undivided attention. One idea I (Richard) used when I worked as a freelance copywriter was the "fifty-minute frenzy." I would set my alarm to give me fifty minutes, then do nothing but write for that entire time. No stopping. No interruptions. It's amazing how much you can get done when you limit interruptions and distractions.

Begin every day with a plan in place. Make your plan the night before. Do your best to stick to your schedule, even when unforeseen things happen that could pull you off track. This will increase your focus and lower your stress as you face the day ahead.

TIME-SAVING TIP #2: EAT THE FROG

No, we are not recommending that you begin a new diet regimen consisting of catching pond creatures for lunch! What we mean by "frog" is the one thing you have been putting off, that one task you'd rather not do. We all have frogs in our lives — activities we would rather not engage in. It could be phone calls or conversations we don't want to have, or paperwork we need to handle.

Whatever your frog is, we strongly suggest that you go ahead and do it first. When we leave important tasks undone, they tend to grow. Our fears make them appear bigger than they actually are. These frogs sap us of the strength and focus we need to accomplish other things. The longer we leave them hanging around, the greater the amount of stress they cause in our lives. Once they are done, no matter how hard or unpleasant they were, we are free to pursue more pleasant activities.

Here are a few of our best "frog-eating" tips:

- *Eat it early.* Get that unpleasant task done as early as possible. If you don't eat it early, it will grow into something much worse. Don't let it grow into a giant mutant frog!

In our time management book, we say that frog-eating is the breakfast of champions. One good reason to eat your frog early is that everything you do after that will be pleasant by comparison.

- *Eat it in manageable bites.* Sometimes the only thing that makes a task a frog is that it is so large. But you don't need to eat the frog all at once. Instead, take that big task and turn it into a bunch of smaller ones. These smaller tasks will almost certainly be easier, and less terrible, than the huge task. Eat it in small bites: break it down into pieces that you can handle so that it doesn't overwhelm you.

- *Be honest about which tasks have become frogs for you.* We all have them, so don't run away from these nasty frogs. Does this task involve dealing with difficult people? Does it cause you to work outside your comfort zone? Do you find yourself putting this task off, hoping it will go away? If the answer to any of these questions is yes, there's a pretty good chance you are facing a frog.

- *Focus your attention on the benefits of eating your frog.* Our fear of the frog can overwhelm us. Our desire to avoid the negative consequences (real or perceived) of tackling the task can make us avoid starting it. Instead of looking at the negatives, concentrate on the positive outcomes you will likely experience when you finish this task. On the other side of this frog is peace, greater unity, and reduced stress.

- *Eat the frog in faith.* There's no reason to let our fears dictate that this unpleasant task will end poorly. We can trust that God is at work, even when we face situations that we would rather avoid. It's tough to keep faith when you are face-to-face with a nasty frog. But remember that God is bigger than all the frogs you face. He is still in control, and you can trust His plan for you.

Frogs are stress-multipliers: if you try to ignore them, they will soon take over all your thoughts and energy. So grab your knife and fork, dive in, and eat that frog!

TIME-SAVING TIP #3: LIVE OFF-PEAK

Most people are creatures of habit. We do the same things, at the same times, on a regular basis. That's fine, but that means a lot of people do identical things at the same times. Most people go to lunch at the same time. They go to the bank at the same time. They go to the movies at certain times.

When large numbers of people decide to do something all at once, it means one thing: waiting. Waiting for a table. Waiting in traffic. Waiting equals wasted time, and wasted time equals stress. For years, I (Nelson) have encouraged my coaching clients to live off-peak.

The main idea of living off-peak is simple: Do things when everyone else is doing something else. Eat an hour before or after the dinner rush. Avoid the bank on Friday afternoon. When you live off-peak, you will find you are waiting far less and using your time much more wisely. That means a lower stress level.

Pastors are in a unique position to live off-peak compared to people in other vocations. Even though we work long, hard hours, our schedules have some flexibility. We can use that flexibility to our advantage and do things at times when others aren't able to. Look for opportunities to use this to your benefit.

Living off-peak is a great way to maximize your use of time! Here are some helpful tips to remember:

- *Remember that different areas have different peaks.* Urban areas have one set of times when the restaurants are busy, while rural areas have another. Resort towns have a whole different set of rules that they live by. Take the time to figure out the peak times in your area so that you can avoid them at all costs.

- *Combine off-peak errands whenever possible.* You can plan to go to the bank and do your grocery shopping all in the same trip. Pick up your dry cleaning on the way out to dinner. When you are able to combine trips, you are not only saving time, you will save money on gas and mileage on your car also. That should result in a lower stress level for you.

- *Automate whenever possible and avoid going out altogether.* A lot of activities can be automated now. You can handle many activities on your phone and skip going out completely. You can automate your banking chores and never go to a bank or credit union. In many areas, you can get your groceries delivered to your door. Tip: Sometimes automating an activity might mean paying a bit more for it. Consider the time savings that you achieve by automating and decide if the extra expense is worth it.

- *Look for off-peak discounts.* Businesses *love* people who come at off-peak hours. It means they are getting money at times when they wouldn't normally have business. Use this to your advantage. Find businesses that offer discounts for customers who use them at off-peak hours. For example, many restaurants offer special dinner discounts for people who dine earlier in the evening. You likely won't have to wait when you go out early, and you get the added benefit of saving some of your hard-earned money. Talk about a stress reliever!

Many average pastors won't think of changing their schedules to live off-peak. But you are not an average pastor. As a Renegade, you are willing to do the unusual to get unusual results. Living off-peak is a great way to make the most of your money and time. And when you use your money and time wisely, you are managing your stress well.

TIME-SAVING TIP #4: DEVELOP EFFECTIVE SYSTEMS FOR YOUR CHURCH

You knew we had to get to the importance of systems at some point in this book. After all, I (Nelson) am sometimes known as the "Church Systems Guy." And there is a reason for that. Healthy systems are vital for pastors who want to grow a healthy church. What I have found is that average pastors resist developing healthy systems, while Renegade Pastors expend the extra effort it takes to build those systems. (And it really doesn't take as much effort as you might think.) The work you put into building systems pays off exponentially in saved time and stress.

In fact, one of my favorite acronyms involves systems. A SYSTEM is something that

Saves
You
Stress
Time
Energy, and
Money

I love this acronym because it reminds us of the value of systems. The investment of time in building the system is nothing compared to the benefit you get from the system being in place. Because this topic is so important, we are going to cover it in some detail.

I have found that there are eight systems in a healthy church: the assimilation system, the evangelism system, the stewardship system, the leadership system, the ministry system, the small groups system, the strategy system, and the worship planning system. When these are in place and working effectively, you usually see a church on the move.

Before we get deeply into the benefits of having healthy systems, we need to be honest about something: setting up effective systems is not easy! It takes time. It takes energy. It might even involve some stress, at the beginning. Even though you see the benefit of installing these systems, not all of your people will be on board, especially when you are starting out. Do not let these things deter you.

Instead of getting bogged down in the difficulties of building systems, keep the big picture in mind. Look at what your church's future can be with these systems in place. Focus on the way these systems can help you build disciples and free those disciples to become the people God created them to be. When you focus on those things, you will understand that the work you are undertaking is worth it.

THE BEST WAY TO BUILD SYSTEMS

You need to exercise wisdom when you are putting systems in place. Otherwise, you will create unnecessary conflict with your congregation. There is no reason to cause yourself, or your church, more stress. Here are some tips on building good systems, learned from the experiences of our churches and churches from all over the world:

- *Go slowly.* When you make the decision to build healthy systems, your natural tendency will be to move quickly. After all, you have the vision of what the future can be. But if you move too quickly, you will encounter more resistance than necessary. Remember, not everyone can see the same future you do. Move slowly, and you will give the people who are resistant an opportunity to catch up to your vision of the way things can be.

- *Keep moving!* Move slowly, but don't stop moving. You will meet some resistance. Some people won't see the need to change. You will encounter other obstacles. The key is to keep making incremental progress every day. Have the necessary tough conversations. Move to the sound of conflict. Even slow progress is better than no progress at all. Slow, steady progress will result in you getting where God wants you to be.

- *Build teams.* Just as you will have people who are resistant to change, you will have some who are early adopters of those changes. These people are the "raving fans" that you need to populate, sustain, and promote your systems. Important: You cannot keep these systems going by yourself. You need other people to carry you through. You are the architect, the visionary, the engine of change. But you need a team — made up of staff and/or volunteers — to help you keep systems going.

- *Start where you will see the biggest impact.* For many churches, I (Nelson) recommend starting with the Assimilation system. There is nothing quite like the shot of electricity that goes through a church when you see guests returning for a second, then a third visit. Seeing those people serve, get saved, and become part of the life of your church will excite your members too. Even small victories can energize a church and motivate your people to make further changes.

- *Keep the big picture in mind.* Building systems can be difficult work. But it is worth it! On the other side of the work you will see the blessing. Keep reminding yourself of what the future holds if you just keep going. And do the same for your congregation. It is easy to lose sight of the vision, especially if you don't see immediate results. Keep plugging away. Don't lose hope. When you build church systems, you are building for a better, lower-stress tomorrow.

We are big believers in the power of systems to relieve stress. (Not to mention all the other benefits that you and your church get from having these systems in place.) And the good news about systems is that I (Nelson) have resources covering every aspect of building and maintaining these essential systems. Learn more at www.RenegadeStressManagement.com. I have in-depth seminars available for each of the eight systems. In these seminars, I go into great detail about how to implement these systems. It's always easi-er to undergo a project like this with a trusted friend, someone who can help you avoid some of the common pitfalls pastors face when they take on this project. My resources can serve as a roadmap as you travel this road — your blueprint for building the systems that your church needs.

Once you have these systems in place, you will really see how they alleviate stress for you. It's like many things in life: The time you in-vest up front putting them together will pay off in better use of your time and a church that is more effective in doing what God has called it to do. And that equals less stress for you.

INVESTING YOUR TIME WELL = MANAGING YOUR STRESS WELL

We hope that you have been able to see just how passionate we are about pastors using time wisely. Often, the one thing that separates average pastors from Renegade Pastors is the way they use their time.

Use your time the way a Renegade Pastor should, and one of the added benefits will be less stress in your life.

One reason that using time wisely decreases stress is that when you use time well, you have more of it. How much more relaxed could you be if you had an extra thirty minutes in your day? Or even an additional hour? You could get more done, get home sooner, spend more time playing with your kids or talking to your spouse. You could pick up a hobby that refreshes your soul. All of this becomes possible when you use time more wisely.

A second, more essential reason why your stress level decreases when you spend time wisely is that it actually brings you closer to God. As we said at the beginning of this chapter, time is the most important resource that God gives us. That means time management is, at its heart, a spiritual issue, a worship issue. Do you show God how much you appreciate His gift of the next moment? One of the best ways to express your appreciation is by getting the most out of every moment He gives you.

We know it can be difficult to change habits that you have developed over the years. If you've never kept a calendar before, it can be hard to start now. Building systems in your church is never easy. It might reveal to you certain people who are resistant to your leadership — people with whom you need to have tough conversations. It might stretch you in ways that you find very uncomfortable. Growth is never easy, and it might be hard to see the benefit, especially in the short term.

But Renegade Pastors are not in ministry for the short term! They know they are in a marathon, not a sprint. You can handle a season of challenges when your eyes are on the future you want to achieve. The goal of time management is not just to handle time well (although that is a worthy goal). The goal is to be a more effective minister to Christ's church. It is to be able to complete the ministry that God has graciously given us.

Stress robs us of the ability to complete a lifetime of effective ministry. And good time management is one tool God has given us to fight stress. Let's use it as we seek to be the pastors God has called us to be!

Chapter 4

PRACTICE POSITIVE SELF-TALK

We take every thought captive to obey Christ.
— 2 Corinthians 10:5

Pastor Alex Average struggles a lot with the stress that comes from within. He is plagued by self-doubt and the persistent fear that he isn't really up to the job. It's like he has a recording running in his mind all the time, telling him that he isn't good enough, that he can't handle the position he is in.

That nagging recording playing in his head causes a great deal of stress for Pastor Alex. It causes him to second-guess his decisions, making him appear indecisive sometimes. At times, he doesn't begin new initiatives at the church because he's convinced that they won't be successful. Worst of all, the negative voice in his head robs him of the joy he should be getting from serving God. It is very difficult to hear the voice of the Spirit when there are other voices competing for Alex's attention.

Pastor Rob Renegade also knows ministry stress. His church is growing, with all the pressures that come from that growth. Sometimes things come up in ministry that Pastor Rob has never encountered before. Yet, he remains positive and upbeat about his ministry.

Like Pastor Alex, Pastor Rob has a voice that he hears repeatedly as he goes throughout his day. But unlike Alex, Rob's recording is constantly reinforcing him. He consistently tells himself that he is up to any challenges he may face. He reminds himself that he has a calling from God to shepherd His people. His mind is filled with Scripture that he has memorized over the years. As a result, Pastor Rob faces a challenging circumstance with the assurance that he is competent to handle it. He knows that God is with him always, and that God will lead him through.

TALKING TO OURSELVES

Sometimes, people hear voices talking to them, even when no one is around. They may even come to believe that there are invisible beings communicating with them. (That is a sign of serious mental illness, and we are definitely not dealing with that subject in this book!)

But all of us "hear voices" all the time. Researchers call it "self-talk," and it is a normal part of life. Self-talk is that ongoing monologue taking place in our minds, either reinforcing positive beliefs about ourselves and our surroundings, or feeding into our negative beliefs about who we are and what we are doing. Because this self-talk is ongoing and pervasive, it is really important that we examine what we are telling ourselves.

Positive self-talk can be a stress-relieving element in our lives. It can keep stress from building up inside ourselves. But negative self-talk can be destructive. Negative self-talk can reinforce defeatist or limiting beliefs we already have about ourselves, which can cause our stress levels to skyrocket.

THE EFFECTS OF NEGATIVE SELF-TALK

It is absolutely true that words alone cannot change reality. But the words we say to ourselves can shape the way we see the world around us. Negative self-talk can harm you in ways that you may not even realize.

In fact, that is one of the ways that negative self-talk becomes so destructive. Because it is constant, we sometimes do not realize what we are saying to ourselves. A never-ending stream of negativity is going through our minds, and we do nothing to stop it. Over time, this can seriously damage our ability to function at the level God intends for us. And that constant flow of negativity has a magnifying effect on our stress level. It's only when we become aware of the negative self-talk going on inside us that we can do something about it.

How does negative self-talk affect us?

- *Negative self-talk lowers our energy level.* When we have those negative thoughts flowing through us, the natural result is going to be a lower energy level. After all, if you are really not up to the challenge, why expend the kind of effort it takes to solve problems?

  This is one of the most destructive aspects of negative self-talk, because it means we don't even try to tackle problems, believing we won't be able to affect positive change anyway. Then this becomes a self-fulfilling prophecy as problems continue to grow without you doing your best to handle them.

- *Negative self-talk leads to procrastination.* If you have a foundational belief that you are not capable of tackling problems, then you won't be anxious to begin the task of solving them. So you put the toughest problems on the back burner, hoping they will go away (which hardly ever happens).

  Here's an example of how this affects you in ministry: If you have a voice in your head that says people don't like talking to you, or that you aren't good with people, how excited are you going to be to interact with guests at your church? You will likely put off those phone calls, visits, or letters, expecting negative results.

- *Negative self-talk causes self-sabotage.* When you believe that you always mess things up, or that you are unlucky, or that God is punishing you for some reason, you will shy away from, or even sabotage, your own success. Many Christians (pastors and non-clergy alike) believe that, for some reason, they are not worthy of God's blessing. So they shy away from the good things that God wants to give them.

My (Richard's) church is deeply involved in helping people recover from drug and alcohol addiction. Unfortunately, I see the effects of this kind of negative self-talk all the time. People believe that because of their past mistakes, they are doomed to a life of addiction. They see the possibility of forgiveness and transformation through Christ, but they just don't think it's possible for them.

- *Negative self-talk can cause you not to take responsibility for the problems in your life and ministry.* If your self-talk is reinforcing the belief that you are a victim, you are not likely to take responsibility for what is going on. And the truth is that we have some responsibility for whatever is happening around us, whether it's good or bad.

This victim's mentality is also something that can cause a great deal of stress. If you consistently see yourself as a victim, you will always be at the mercy of the next thing that happens. If, however, you see yourself as strong and competent, you will be able to fight against the negative things that happen to all of us. We must take responsibility and act in faith to solve problems we encounter.

- *Negative self-talk can damage our faith in God.* If you have a voice constantly telling you that you aren't good enough, or that you are doomed to failure, you are likely to start to doubt God's goodness. And your faith will suffer.

As pastors, we must exhibit the traits that we tell our congregation about. We cannot talk about our people growing in faith when our own faith is lacking. And, just as importantly, we won't attempt great things for God if we don't truly believe in His goodness or faithfulness toward us.

HOW NEGATIVE SELF-TALK AFFECTS YOUR CONGREGATION

In this book we are talking especially to pastors. But there are many people in our congregations who suffer from the effects of negative self-talk. We all can probably name people who believe they aren't capable, or that God is punishing them for something they did earlier in life. With those negative thoughts, there's no doubt their stress levels are higher than they ought to be.

If we can get control of our own self-talk, we can be a major blessing to these people who may not even realize they are suffering. We can teach them by our own example that they can gain control over their thought life and experience more from the life that they currently have.

NEGATIVE SELF-TALK IS UNBIBLICAL

At its very core, negative self-talk is unbiblical for a number of reasons. We need to recognize it and fight against it with everything we have!

- *Negative self-talk speaks against God's goodness.* Does God really work all things for our good (Rom. 8:28)? Not if you believe the negative thoughts in your head. We can't keep any thoughts that don't acknowledge God's essential love and goodness.

- *Negative self-talk degrades God's creation.* Even though we are all sinful and flawed, we are also all creations of God. As Christians, we are God's new creation (2 Cor. 5:17) saved for a purpose (Eph. 2:10). Those are facts, and negative self-talk causes us to forget what they mean for us.

- *Negative self-talk weakens our faith.* We talked about this at length earlier, so we won't go into detail about it now. But, without faith, it is impossible to please God (Heb. 11:6). Any talk that weakens our faith in God is something to be avoided at all costs!

WELL-INTENTIONED NEGATIVITY

For some of us, our natural default position is to have negative self-talk. It may be due to our childhood. We may have heard these negative messages from our parents or from other family members. Sometimes people put this negative recording in our heads with good intentions.

Many of us have told our kids something like, "You shouldn't try that! It's too hard for you!" Or, "There's no way you will be able to do THAT!" Our intention may have been to prepare our kids for the possibility that they might fail. But those words can become the soundtrack to our children's lives. Our kids may internalize that message and begin to believe it's true in every circumstance.

PAST FAILURES RESURFACING

Some of us come from hard places, maybe because of our own poor choices. God saved us from a lifestyle of sin and addiction, and set us on a new road. But, as we said earlier, when you are in those dark places, you can start to believe some negative things about yourself. You can find your self-talk reflecting the person you used to be, before God saved you and called you according to His purpose. When that happens, you can limit yourself and even limit God's blessing in your life.

PRACTICING POSITIVE SELF-TALK

If you are one of the many Christians — even Christian leaders — who find themselves plagued by negative self-talk, you are in good company. This is a malady that plagues many of us. The key is to not be content or satisfied with where we are, or with that negative voice that keeps talking to us. Instead, we need to reprogram that voice. We need to teach ourselves to think and speak in positive, reaffirming, faith-building, stress-reducing ways. It takes work, but it is possible, and we will be glad we made the effort.

A word of caution as you begin to re-record the messages you tell yourself: this will not always be easy. If you have been in negative self-talk mode for your entire life, you won't change overnight. Those voices have been in your head for a long time, and they feel like they are at home. It will take concerted effort, time, and repeated struggle to evict those voices from your head. But the truth is, they don't belong in your head anyway. They need to be gone!

The problem isn't so much that those voices feel like they are at home, telling you negative things that aren't true about yourself. The real problem is that we start to believe these voices, and *we* think they have a legitimate home in our thoughts and attitudes. We get too comfortable with this negative recording. After all, we have been hearing it our whole lives, in many cases. It must be true.

Except that it isn't true at all. Those negative voices may be comfortable for us. They may feel normal to us. But in reality, they are just lies that the devil tells believers to keep them from reaching the place where God wants them to be. As Renegade Pastors, we need to recognize these tools of Satan, root them out, and learn to live in the light of God's positive thoughts about us.

GOD'S TRUTH IS POSITIVE

Learning positive self-talk is not about believing something that just isn't true. It isn't about buying into some self-help mumbo jumbo that you might hear from a TV talk show. Instead, positive self-talk that Renegade Pastors use is grounded in the very real words and promises of God. We believe that God is extremely positive about His children, and we should share God's thinking on this.

That's an important distinction, because none of us will listen for very long to words that we know aren't true. We may want to believe something, but if it doesn't fit in with truth as defined by God, we will eventually leave it behind, realizing that it's just wishful thinking. After all, we would never encourage our congregations to listen to something that wasn't true. That's why we are advocating a type of self-talk that *is* true, as well as being uplifting and positive.

A PARTICULAR BRAND OF SELF-TALK

Being a pastor is a special calling from God. If it weren't, it might not be worth going through all we have to endure to do the job of leading God's people. Since it is a special calling, with its own set of problems and challenges, we need to have the best, most God-honoring self-talk going on in our heads. What are the advantages of changing the recording in our heads? Here are a few:

- *Greater faith in God.* If we see God as He really is — in all His mercy and goodness — and recognize all that He has done for us, we will naturally see our faith increase. He wants us to trust Him and to know that He is working all things out for our good. Our self-talk should reinforce that!

Negative self-talk says, "Maybe God isn't worthy of being trusted!" It can cause us to doubt, even if we don't consciously realize it. The right kind of self-talk reinforces God's essential goodness and His willingness to work on our behalf.

- *A positive view of ourselves.* As human beings, we walk between two truths about ourselves. We are, at the same time, sinful, flawed creatures, and also God's special creation. We are a combination of many good gifts from God and a sinful nature that trips us up.

  The problem comes for us when we emphasize the sinful, flawed aspect of ourselves to the detriment of what God has done, and continues to do, in us. We should be aware of our sinful nature, while at the same time reminding ourselves repeatedly of all we have, and are, in Christ.

- *Increased energy for ministry.* If your head is filled with negative thoughts, even if those thoughts appear normal, you will find your energy level decreasing. After all, if you are not capable and worthy of solving ministry problems, then what's the point of trying? You expect a negative result before you even get started.

  Positive self-talk, on the other hand, is energizing. You can tackle problems with gusto, knowing that there is nothing you and God can't handle. When you begin to remind yourself of how many talents God has blessed you with, you know that you can use those talents to solve any problems that come your way.

- *A great example for your congregation.* Most people who struggle with negative self-talk don't have good role models to show them how to change the way they feel about themselves. You can provide that role model. As you change, you can show others how they can change also.

  This is one of the many areas where people need to be shown the truth and not just preached to. People are always more likely to follow our example. As Renegade Pastors, we should be at the forefront: teaching ourselves to think truthfully about who we are in Christ, and leading our congregations to do the same.

- *Decreased ministry stress.* When you change your way of thinking, it will make a huge difference in your life. Your beliefs about who God is will change for the better. Your beliefs about who you are will also change for the better. You will see that you are more than capable of tackling whatever comes your way.

  It just follows that if you realize you are capable of handling anything that comes your way, your stress level will naturally decrease. There's no reason to be overly stressed, because you and God have everything under control. That is a great feeling, and it comes when you re-record your self-talk.

NOT JUST ANY SELF-TALK

We don't recommend that you just try to be more positive, to have a happier outlook on life. Those negative thoughts have been at home in your head for so long that they won't leave simply because you're thinking happy thoughts. You need to bring out the heavy artillery to destroy that ingrained negative self-talk.

We have found that the most effective tool for changing your internal dialogue is the Bible. God's Word contains all the truth we need to live as believers in Christ. And that truth, for God's children, is overwhelmingly positive. We need to keep our hearts and minds saturated with the truth of Scripture if we are going to successfully fight against the negative self-talk that plagues us. When we fill our mind with Scripture, we find our recordings changing naturally, bringing our thoughts in line with God's Word.

As we have said before, many of us have been practicing negative self-talk for our entire lives. We are really good at it, even though it is hurtful and destructive. If we are going to change the way we talk to ourselves, we need to have a strategy in place. So, how do we change the way we think and engage in positive self-talk? We suggest these three steps:

Step #1: Notice the Way You Talk to Yourself
Since these negative thoughts are likely deeply rooted in your thinking, you may not even realize you have them. In order to change, you need to realize what you are actually saying to yourself. When you are facing a troubling issue, notice what you are thinking. Are you assuming the worst or downgrading your ability to take care of the problem at hand? Are you doubting God's ability to work in your life and ministry? Be careful to notice what you are thinking.

To be more aware of the thoughts in your head, you may want to consider writing them down. Keeping a journal of what you are thinking can help you see, in writing, what your thoughts are. That will also help you to recall your thoughts as you reflect on them at a later time.

Step #2: Stop the Negative Thought

Once you realize that you are thinking negatively, train yourself to stop before that thought can take hold and become rooted in your thinking. The longer you let that thought just sit there, the harder it will be to get rid of it. So act quickly.

There are many good ways to stop a negative thought. One is to just say "Stop!" either to yourself or out loud. That is a great way to reinforce the fact that you are not going to tolerate those thoughts any longer. A second tactic for stopping a negative thought is to wear a rubber band around your wrist. When you realize you are having a negative or limiting thought, snap the rubber band to remind yourself to stop.

Whatever method you choose, the important thing is to stop a negative thought as soon as you realize it's in your head. But stopping a thought isn't enough. We need something to replace it with.

Step #3: Replace the Thought with a Truth from Scripture

God intends for Scripture to be relevant to every aspect of our lives, so there is a Scripture for every predicament we might face. Are you doubting God's work in your life? Try Romans 8:28 as an antidote. Not seeing God's plan in a scenario? Maybe Genesis 50:20 will help. Wondering if God will provide for you when you're facing a tough spot? Philippians 4:13 speaks to that. Not sure God is still working in your life? Try Philippians 1:6.

It's a good idea to memorize as much Scripture as possible, and this is one of the reasons why. When you have those Scriptures memorized, you can apply them quickly in any given situation. When they are already in your memory, they can transfer quickly to your thinking.

Once you start applying Scripture to the circumstances you face, your thoughts change. You become more positive, more confident, more able to fulfill the calling God has on your life, and less stressed out by the problems every pastor faces. We cannot stress highly enough how important this is. Getting control of your thoughts can literally change your ministry.

God never promised that we would have stress-free lives. In fact, He promised that in this world, we would have troubles (John 16:33). But He also promised that He would walk with us through all of them. When we clear our thoughts of the cluttered negativity that fill our minds, we give Him space to work, space to move.

In order to be the Renegade Pastor that we know you want to be (and that God has called you to be), you need to say goodbye to the negative, limiting, defeatist thoughts that fill your mind so easily. Those thoughts make you look through a filter that casts everything in a negative light. When you replace those thoughts with God-honoring ones, you see the world more clearly, the way God sees it.

It definitely takes work to change our self-talk. Lifetime habits are not easily broken! And these habits they must be constantly replaced, so they are not allowed to come back. But if you take the time and effort to engage in positive self-talk, we know that you will find God working in you and through you in ways you haven't seen before. Replace that negative recording with words straight from God.

Chapter 5

TAKE MINI-BREAKS

Yet (Jesus) often withdrew to deserted places and prayed.
— Luke 5:16

If there is one word that describes Pastor Alex Average, that word is *busy*. He takes his calling as a pastor very seriously. He never takes the responsibility and privilege of leading God's people for granted. Yet his work is never-ending; there is no way he can possibly do all that is required of him.

So Pastor Alex gets worn down, almost on a daily basis. He finds that when he gets tired, he has a lower level of energy. His mind isn't as sharp as it needs to be to accomplish what he needs to do. Alex realizes this, and that causes him more stress in his ministry and home life. He wishes that he could be less tired, more focused, and more energetic.

Pastor Rob Renegade also knows what it means to be busy. He knows ministry is difficult, but he also has learned how to handle the stress. He thrives in spite of the stress. People know that when a decision needs to be made, Pastor Rob can be trusted to act with clarity, conviction, and wisdom.

His family loves him. They know something of the pressures of his job. They know he works long hours, and that isn't likely to change anytime soon. But they also know that when he is with them, he is really with them. He stays clear and level-headed throughout the day and night. As a result, his home life is thriving. And because he isn't worried about his family, his stress level is very manageable.

Pastor Rob Renegade has discovered something that he credits with revolutionizing his life and ministry: he rests for brief periods throughout the day. It sounds counterintuitive, but he finds that these mini-breaks are an essential part of his vitality. He has the same mood and energy swings that everybody has. But he finds that he can deal with those better because he is willing to take a few minutes every day to shut everything down and rest. Because he is better rested, when he gets home, his family gets the best of him, not just what he has left over. Rob is a better, more productive person because he takes time to rest.

THE IMPORTANCE OF TAKING MINI-BREAKS

We want to warn you at the outset: much of what we will talk about in this chapter will appear to contradict what you have heard about being productive. But we, and many productivity experts, will tell you that we are right on target with the advice we are about to give you.

Many of us have bought into the idea that the only way to be really productive is to work every moment of the day. In this view, inaction equals laziness and doesn't help us at all with getting things done. I (Nelson) always advise my coaching clients to be people who take action. One of my favorite sayings is "Run toward conflict." Problems rarely get better until we take action.

There is a growing body of evidence that shows us it is important to find time to rest during the day. Now, we realize that this flies in the face of what we have traditionally believed about work. Most of us were taught that in order to be a good worker you need to be the first person in the office in the morning and the last to leave at night. The people who did that were the best employees, the ones who provided the most value for their company — and the ones who got ahead in life. But we understand better today, and we know that working harder and longer isn't necessarily the best way to get things done.

This is important, because working harder and longer brings with it some rather unpleasant side effects: high stress levels, no time for family, and an out-of-balance life. Then there are the health effects of overworking: obesity, heart disease, and all the related chronic illnesses. These diseases and ill effects can be largely avoided if we learn to take strategic mini-breaks.

At this point, you might be wondering, "How does taking mini-breaks fit in with this idea of taking action? You can't be on break and taking action at the same time!" And, in one sense, that is completely true. We Renegade Pastors need to be people who take faith-filled action whenever it becomes necessary. But we don't believe that the idea of taking breaks conflicts with this idea. In fact, we think mini-breaks make you better able to take effective action.

The key to what we are going to outline in this chapter is to take strategic mini-breaks. We are not endorsing sleeping an extra hour every day or spending less time in the office. (Although we do cover those subjects in the chapter on rest, later in this book.) We understand that sometimes the best, most effective thing you can do is to step away from your work and take time to recharge.

HEALTH BENEFITS OF MINI-BREAKS

Taking mini-breaks is a great way to reduce your stress level and get more done at work at the same time. In fact, a recent study done by a group of researchers from Baylor University found a number of surprising benefits that happened when workers took mini-breaks throughout the day:[1]

- *Higher levels of job satisfaction.* People who take breaks during the day typically enjoy their job more than those who don't. Think how important that can be when you are dealing with challenging people and circumstances. When you enjoy what you do, it makes the hard times easier to bear. When you enjoy your job, it is easier to remember that it's more than a job — it's a calling from God.

- *Reduced emotional exhaustion.* Every pastor, even a Renegade Pastor, knows that the occupation wears you down. But when you take mini-breaks, you have the opportunity to recharge during the day. You never get overly-depleted or emotionally exhausted. This keeps you moving forward on tough days.

- *More willingness to take on difficult projects.* When you take mini-breaks, you take the opportunity to recharge emotionally and physically, as we said earlier. When you are refreshed, you have more energy, and your outlook is more positive. Those factors feed your faith, and you will find that you are more willing to take on those tasks that you may be procrastinating on.

As you can see, this study suggests that you will see a number of positive results from taking strategic mini-breaks. To make time for mini-breaks, you may need to rearrange your schedule a bit. But that work will be worth it when you are more relaxed, have more clarity and focus, experience more energy, and enjoy a positive outlook on your ministry.

We find that many pastors resist the idea of taking breaks — even once they understand how they could benefit from adopting the practice. After all, it's something new. It means that you will need to do something differently, which can be scary and uncomfortable. And it goes against what we have heard from our earliest days. That kind of resistance may provide an acceptable excuse for average pastors to shy away from trying it. But you, as a Renegade, know that anything that cuts our stress level is worth pursuing — even if it means going against the grain.

WHAT'S NEEDED IS A CHANGE OF THINKING

Any time we are exposed to something that challenges our preconceived ideas, it takes courage to adopt it. In this case, the idea that we need breaks certainly goes against the concept of the hard-working person laboring from sunrise to sunset. We need to change our way of thinking in this area.

It will take time for this practice to feel comfortable for you. While it does, we have two suggestions that will help you persevere in doing something you haven't done before:

First, look at the benefits of your new behavior. Evaluate your effectiveness, your focus, your energy. Are you seeing the benefits of taking breaks? If you are, let that motivate you to keep moving forward.

Next, see how this idea can benefit your congregation. Many people in our churches are literally working themselves to death. You can share with them the value of resting. (In the next chapter we expand on the idea of rest and apply these principles to your entire life and ministry.)

WHAT KIND OF BREAKS SHOULD YOU TAKE?

As you probably expect, not just any type of break will reenergize you. You need to be intentional and strategic if you want to get the maximum benefit from this practice. So let's look at the "rules" that make for better breaks:

- *Actually take breaks.* A 2012 study found that only one in five workers in corporate life takes breaks on a regular basis.[2] Do not be one of the 80% percent! Instead, make it part of your regular schedule to take time to recharge. You, and your congregation, will be very glad you did!

- *Take two ten-to-fifteen-minute breaks per day.* Researchers found that this is an optimum number of breaks. In a traditional job, breaks are usually before and after lunch — which is a great way to plan your day. There is little or no added benefit to taking more breaks, which is an area we will cover later in this chapter.

There is also no research that indicates that longer breaks are better. At some point, taking extra time actually hurts you. It causes you to lose focus and forget what you are working on. Plus, you do need sufficient time to work during the day.

- *Take your morning break early in your work day.* The Baylor University study was clear: It's better to take your morning break earlier, rather than closer to lunch. Workers who took breaks later in the morning reported more fatigue, more aches and pains, and a lower energy level, even after their break was over.

A better plan is to spread your breaks out evenly throughout the day. Take your morning break rather early, followed by lunch, and then the afternoon break. This timing enables you to get the most out of your breaks.

- *Healthy snacks are your friend.* Many people make the mistake of eating fatty, sugary, unhealthy snacks during their breaks. Admit it: all of us have eaten a bag of chips and downed it with a soda during our breaks. It's normal to get hungry at break time, and it's usually not hard to find something to eat that is terrible for you.

Here's the problem: that snack that is loaded with fat and sugar is the worst thing you can eat on your break. Not only do those snacks contribute to your obesity, they make you sleepy and sap your energy. In addition, they mess with your appetite, making you hungry later on in the day.

Fruits and vegetables make for much better snacks. They satiate your hunger while actually increasing your energy level. They give you the nutrients your body is craving so that it can operate the way God created it to. (For more information on how good nutrition can help you have a more effective ministry, read the book I [Nelson] wrote with Steve Reynolds, *The Healthy Renegade Pastor*.)

- *Do something you enjoy during your break*. If you want to spend your fifteen minutes staring at the wall, we think that's okay. If that helps you recharge, go for it. But there are much better ways to invest your break time.

Our first suggestion for your break time is to get out and take a walk. I (Nelson) said it in my book *The Healthy Renegade Pastor* and I'll say it again here: Christians are the fattest people group in America. And pastors are the fattest Christians! That shouldn't be true, but it is. We need to take care of our physical bodies. It's vital for our long-term ministry effectiveness.

So, spend that fifteen minutes taking a walk outside. The physical activity will improve your outlook. Your body will thank you. You might even start on the road to getting healthy!

Second, breathe. This one sounds ridiculously easy. After all, we have been breathing our whole lives (hopefully!). But this isn't as easy as it sounds. Most of us don't breathe correctly, and this adds to our stress level. It also decreases our energy and focus. Correct breathing technique is often a vital key to good health.

Slow, deep breathing has many health benefits. It can help you clear your head of all the clutter and trivia that gets stuck in there. This type of breathing gets plenty of oxygen into your system, en-suring your lungs, and even your cells, have the fuel they need to perform at peak efficiency. Some experts believe that proper breathing can result in fifteen more toxins being flushed out of your system, compared to poor, shallow breathing.

So, how do you practice proper breathing? Start with this ten-minute exercise: Get as relaxed as you can. Lie flat on a couch if possible; otherwise, sit up in a comfortable chair. Close your eyes and notice any areas of tension in your body. Try to let that tension go, as much as possible.

Practice breathing through your nose. Take long breaths, concentrating on filling your lower abdomen with air. Don't breathe quickly; just allow the air into your body. Many people make the mistake of inhaling too quickly. Don't do that. Focus on taking long, slow breaths.

After doing this for about ten minutes, you should feel significantly more relaxed, focused, and energetic. This is a great break-time exercise. But your goal should be to breathe this way all the time! Throughout the day, you should periodically check your breathing. Concentrate on breathing more slowly and more deeply. You will see the benefits.

Third, we think you should read on your breaks. By read, we don't mean just reading books on ministry or pastoral care. Read something that's relaxing, like a mystery novel. Anything you find entertaining will work. All leaders are readers, but save your ministry-related reading for your work time. During your breaks, keep it light!

Fourth, sleep. Take a ten- or fifteen-minute nap. You don't need to sleep longer than that to reap the benefits. Just a little nap can give you more energy, improve your clarity and focus, and increase your productivity.

We know that many of you will find it difficult to incorporate the idea of sleeping or resting during the day. It will seem odd, too odd to handle, for many of you. But keep in mind the benefit you are getting from this rest: it is well worth it!

Last, meditate on Scripture. We probably don't need to tell you how important it is that you fill your heart and mind with God's Word. Spend some of your break time memorizing Scripture. This is in addition to your regular devotional time and also in addition to your sermon preparation. Time you spend in God's Word is indeed time well spent.

Of course, you should include prayer in your meditation time. We like to think of prayer and Bible meditation as two parts of a conversation with God. We hear from God through His Word, and He hears from us as we pray to Him. The practice of meditating on Scripture, beyond our normal devotional time, will make a big difference in our stress level and our ministry effectiveness.

BREAK ACTIVITIES YOU SHOULD AVOID

Those are all great ideas for how you should spend your break time. Unfortunately, it is really easy to fall into some bad habits during your breaks. The problem with the activities we are about to talk about is not so much that they are time-wasters (which they certainly are). The problem is that they are counterproductive. You will come back from your break feeling less energetic and more stressed — the complete opposite of what you are trying to achieve. So here are a few things to avoid when you are taking a strategic mini-break:

- *Avoid eating fatty or sugary foods.* This is the flip side of the tip we gave you earlier about snacking on fruits and vegetables. We all know the types of foods we are talking about: cakes, cookies, chips, and ice cream. These foods taste so good when you eat them, but what they do to your body is anything but beneficial. They make you sluggish and slow. They probably will increase your cravings for high-fat foods later in the day. Stay away from these foods at all costs.

This principle applies to our lunch break as well. When we choose to fill our bodies with fast food that is high-fat and high-calorie, we are setting ourselves up for a less-productive, higher-stress afternoon. Our bodies have to work harder just to digest all that garbage we have ingested. The extra effort our bodies use takes away from our normal energy levels. So for a productive afternoon, eat light at lunch.

Another word of caution about what you put in your body: some of the drinks we consume are just as bad as the foods we eat. Sodas are nothing but sugar (and diet sodas may not be much better for you). And many of the popular coffee drinks are extremely high in sugar and calories. Be aware of what you are eating and drinking.

- *Avoid skipping lunch altogether.* It's very tempting to skip eating and just work through lunch. Don't do it unless you are engaged in a period of fasting. (If you would like to know more about fasting, I [Nelson] have a resource called *Fasting for Spiritual Breakthrough*, which teaches you the basics of fasting. Download it for free at www.RenegadeStressManagement.com When you don't eat, it can have a similar effect to eating the wrong things — sluggishness, lack of energy and focus, and intense hunger.

As we said in the last point, the key is to eat strategically. Eat a light lunch, with an emphasis on lean meats, fruits, and vegetables. When you choose to eat this way, two things happen. First, your body doesn't need to work as hard to digest the food, which frees up more energy for you to concentrate on your work. Second, these types of food provide the proper fuel your body craves. When you give your body what it wants and needs, it performs better.

- *Avoid checking email and social media.* We live in a world where are connected to each other constantly, in ways that we never were before the Internet came into existence. But it is very easy to let email and social media become time-wasters. And they can not only steal your time, they can destroy your energy level also.

  We have all been there: You sit down to check Facebook "just for a minute." When you look up, two hours have passed, and you haven't accomplished anything. Make your breaks a respite from the ever-present draw of social media. This simple change can make a big difference in your life!

  In our book *The Renegade Pastor's Guide to Time Management* (available at Amazon.com), we suggest that you schedule the time you spend on both email and social media. That way you are in control of how and when that time is spent, rather than having those activities control you.

- *Avoid the "one little thing" syndrome.* We're sure you've fallen prey to this. We certainly have. It's the temptation to just look at "one little thing" or take some small bit of work with you on your break. Resist this temptation! Those "little things" can be time and energy vampires, sucking you dry.

- *Avoid taking too many breaks, or breaks that are too long.* It doesn't take much to recharge our emotional and physical batteries. Most Renegade Pastors love what they do, and they are fine if they confine themselves to these strategic breaks. If you use breaks the way we suggest, you shouldn't have any problems with focus, energy, or productivity during the day.

Something else to keep in mind is that taking too many breaks can actually be bad for you. You need to be engaged and alert when you are at work, and long breaks can interfere with that. Use breaks in moderation so you receive the maximum benefit from them.

A PRACTICE YOU SHOULDN'T LIVE WITHOUT

Sometimes we decide not to try something because it's new or goes against what we have heard or been taught. This idea of taking mini-breaks may be one of those new ideas that you may not be comfortable with. Don't let that get in your way! You need this practice to be part of your schedule.

After all, which of us Renegade Pastors would say no to something that will reduce our stress level as well as increase our energy and focus — plus give us the vigor we need to be the spouse and parent we want to be? Just remember to break strategically, keeping these things in mind:

- *Breaks help you only if you actually take them.* Don't skip breaks — they are too important for you to miss!

- *Two ten-to-fifteen-minute breaks per day is all you need to refresh and recharge.* More than that is too much. These two breaks, along with lunch, is plenty.

- *Take your morning break early.* Research shows that an early break is more relaxing and reduces both stress and physical pain.

- *Eat healthy snacks.* High-fat and high-sugar snacks (or meals) are bad for you, hard to digest, and lower your focus and energy level.

- *Do something you enjoy on your break.* This can include any number of things, like taking a walk, practicing deep breathing, eating healthy snacks, reading for pleasure, taking a nap, and praying and meditating on Scripture.

If you use your breaks in this way, you will see an increase in your energy level. You will notice that your focus is better throughout the day. You will make better decisions. When you go home after a long day, you will be a better spouse and parent. In short, taking mini-breaks will make you a better pastor and increase the impact of your ministry. Make mini-breaks a regular part of your schedule.

Chapter 6

TAKE CARE OF YOURSELF PHYSICALLY

Don't you realize that your body is the temple of the Holy Spirit, who lives in you and was given to you by God? You do not belong to yourself, for God bought you with a high price. So you must honor God with your body.

1 CORINTHIANS 6:19-20

Pastor Alex Average is concerned. He works long hours taking care of church business. Now he can't help but notice that he isn't quite as lean as he used to be. In fact, he has put on about forty pounds since he came to the church fifteen years ago. It's not so much that he eats *a lot* of food. He just eats a little too much. And his attempts at regular exercise have been, well, less than regular. He does try to get aerobic exercise — he knows how important it is — but his efforts often fall short. Those long hours he works eat up his exercise time in many cases.

Pastor Alex, who is now in his late 40s, recognizes something that most people don't see yet: his energy level is slowly decreasing. He is tired more often as he ages. He is not often sick. But when he gets sick, it takes a toll on him. The stress of ministry is also taking its toll. For Pastor Alex, the worst part of losing energy is certainly this: he can see that if his energy level keeps decreasing, his ministry fruitfulness will also decrease. He doesn't like to think about slowing down, but he can see it happening.

Pastor Rob Renegade has more energy than any of his staff. He can outwork them all. He has a great vision for what God has called his church to be, and he works hard to make that vision a reality. He and his staff work regular hours. At Pastor Rob's direction, his staff leaves time in their schedules for family, and also for exercise. He himself is an avid exerciser. He runs almost every morning. He lifts weights two to three times per week. He credits his exercise routine with helping him stay in shape physically and keeping him sharp mentally and spiritually.

For Rob, it is a challenge to eat right on his job, but he does well. (Not perfectly, but well.) Pastor Rob sees many benefits from being physically fit and active. He knows that his energy and focus are tied to his physical health. The fact that he is rarely sick is also due to his good physical health.

Perhaps most important for Pastor Rob is what he sees in his future. He doesn't see the same kind of energy decline that other pastors experience at his age. He knows that he is going to be able to keep working hard to fulfill his calling for as long as God has him in ministry. He won't have to leave for a position that carries less authority and less stress, because he knows he will be able to handle whatever comes his way.

TAKING CARE OF THE OTHER PART OF US

It's safe to say that, as a culture, we are obsessed with our physical bodies. We spend billions of dollars on beauty aids, books on health and fitness, and nutritional supplements. We spend countless amounts on exercise equipment and gym memberships. We act committed, as a society, to taking care of our physical bodies.

But as pastors, we are different. We have a completely different set of priorities, a higher focus. We are concerned with our own spiritual lives and the spiritual lives of those around us. We understand that our earthly bodies are temporary, that no matter how much care we take of our physical bodies, they will one day die. Meanwhile, our spirits live forever. As pastors, our calling is to nurture that eternal, spiritual part of our congregation.

We completely agree that our focus needs to be on growing and feeding our spiritual lives. But we also know how important it is to take care of our bodies. In fact, we don't think it's an either/or proposition, where we must choose between our bodies and our spirits, as though we can nurture only one or the other. We firmly believe that you can — you *should* — nurture both your spirit and your body, along with your mind as well. In fact, we believe it's a sin to solely focus on one aspect of ourselves to the neglect of the others.

PASTORING THE WHOLE PERSON

You see, we are amazing creations of God, creations that cannot be separated into neat little compartments. When one part of us suffers, we suffer in every area. In particular, when we don't feel well physically, we get dragged down mentally, emotionally, and spiritually. We find our energy level decreasing simply because our bodies can't keep up the frantic pace of ministry. When we don't feel well, we can't handle stress well. And our whole ministry suffers as a result.

Many pastors we know just don't take the time to take care of themselves physically. They figure that they can maintain their effectiveness in ministry by staying strong spiritually, emotionally, and mentally. But what happens far too often is that we neglect our bodies, and soon our minds aren't as sharp. We find that we can't absorb some of the emotional shocks that come as a pastor. Our desire to learn and grow is dampened, all because we have neglected our bodies. The result? A shortened, less effective, less joyful ministry — a ministry that falls short of what God wants it to be.

We run the very real risk as pastors of missing out on some of God's greatest blessings simply because we don't take care of ourselves. We all know the statistics of how many pastors leave their positions every year. One reason pastors quit is that they just can't handle the stress of ministry. And taking care of your body is a key component to handling stress effectively.

I (Nelson) went through the statistics in detail in the book *The Healthy Renegade Pastor*, which I wrote with pastor Steve Reynolds (available through Amazon.com). Christians are the most physically unhealthy people group in the world. Rates of obesity, heart disease, diabetes, and other lifestyle-related ailments are much higher among Christians than in the general population.

And, unfortunately, pastors lead this unhealthy parade. We pay the price for our lack of physical health. Having a fit, healthy spirit does not ensure that we will not suffer the effects of an unhealthy lifestyle. Too many pastors suffer from heart disease, diabetes, and other ailments due to their neglect of their bodies.

But Renegade Pastors don't follow this trend. They know how important it is to stay healthy and fit — spiritually, intellectually, emotionally, and physically. It is only with this kind of commitment to the whole person that the Renegade Pastor will find true fulfillment and fruitfulness in their calling. We want to be everything God has called us to be. The only way to do that is to take care of the body He has given us.

THE EFFECTS OF BAD HEALTH

We have already talked a bit about what happens to us as pastors when we do not take care of ourselves physically. In this section, we spell out what happens when pastors refuse to get and stay healthy.

- *We lose energy and passion for ministry — and life.* It isn't just the fact that we lose the energy we need to accomplish ministry tasks. We lose the energy to do many of the things we love to do. It will affect our pastoral work, of course. But the lack of energy will also show up when we spend time with our families. We will probably end up feeling like we are cheating our kids and spouses out of the best part of ourselves.

- *We lose the vision of what God has called us to do.* When we don't feel our best, our thinking gets muddled. We don't see as clearly either. We particularly lose sight of the great vision we once had for what God has called us to do. We pastors must maintain a clear vision of what God is calling us to. If we lose that vision, we risk losing a key piece of God's call for our ministry. To keep that clear vision, we need sound thinking — and that means we need a healthy body.

- *We become a bad example of what God expects from His servants.* God does not want His servants run into the ground by the stress of ministry. When we refuse to take the time needed to take care of ourselves physically, we in essence tell our congregations, "God is going to use you until you're used up, then He's done with you." Of course, we don't want our congregations to have that view of God. When we take care of ourselves, we show that God loves and cares for every part of us.

- *We face the very real prospect of a shortened ministry career.* We are convinced that health concerns have taken out thousands of pastors before their time. Pastors who had to quit to pursue less demanding jobs based on their doctor's advice. Pastors who had to retire early because they had serious medical conditions. But there is something special about a pastor who has stayed the course for thirty, forty, fifty years or more. They have a depth of wisdom that can't be matched. That's the kind of pastor we want you to be.

- *We dishonor God Himself.* How can we pastors dishonor God? When we neglect our physical health, we are telling God that we don't care about one aspect of His creation. Remember that your body, no matter what kind of shape it's in, is still a gift given to you by God. You get only one of them per lifetime. We know that our bodies are temporary, but we need to take care of them to the best of our ability.

These are just a few of the effects of neglecting yourself physically. But these should be enough to motivate you to make some changes. Change is not easy. If you feel locked into old habits of feeding your mind and soul while not paying enough attention to your body, then let this section persuade you to adjust your practices.

- *When we take care of our bodies, we experience a renewed energy and excitement.* When I (Richard) decided to get healthy a few years ago, I wasn't ready for the surge of energy I experienced. I found that people fifteen years younger than I am had trouble keeping up with me. People who don't know how old I am regularly guess that I'm a decade younger than I actually am. Talk about a confidence booster!

- *When we take care of our bodies, our families receive a blessing also.* You are not the only one who pays a price when you are not healthy. Your family pays the price of having a tired, stressed-out, sick spouse and parent. So getting healthy is not just for you — it's for your family as well. Don't rob your family. Instead, give them the best gift of all: the gift of your healthy, energetic presence in their lives.

- *When we take care of our bodies, ministry — and everything else — becomes more enjoyable.* Being healthy gives you the ability to handle problems and stress much more effectively. That leads to greater joy. We can't eliminate problems. But physical health is key to personal joy and satisfaction. In addition, when you feel better, you have a greater sense of optimism — which makes you better able to handle stress.

- *When we take care of our bodies, we set a proper example for our congregation.* As we said before, Christians are the most out-of-shape people group around. How are Christians supposed to learn to take care of themselves if their pastors can't show them the way? We want to be leaders in a healthy revolution.

THE TWO KEYS TO GETTING (AND STAYING) PHYSICALLY FIT

Before we get into some specific strategies that will help you take better care of the body God has given you, we need to issue a warning. We are pastors, and we think we are pretty good ones! But neither of us are doctors. So we can't give you medical advice. Before you make any lifestyle changes, you need to go see your doctor. Make sure he or she knows what you have in mind, and get his or her approval before doing anything. (We have found that most doctors will be thrilled that you are getting serious about your physical health. They will likely have some good suggestions and will become some of your biggest supporters!)

Once you get your doctor on board, we recommend some simple but profound changes. These changes will give you a much greater amount of energy and positivity. They will lower your stress and give you a greater joy for ministry.

In reality, there are two areas where you probably need to make changes in order to be in better health — exercise and diet.

THE FIRST KEY: EXERCISE

We always chuckle when we see pictures of Jesus that depict Him as a small, frail European-looking man, a man who looks like He couldn't hurt a fly, even if He wanted to. The truth is that the men of Jesus' day, especially those from the working classes, were far tougher than many of us are today.

Jesus was the son of a carpenter and learned carpentry skills at the feet of His father, Joseph. This was long before the days of power tools, and carpentry was backbreaking work. (It still is!) They carried their wood, and the tools of their trade, everywhere they worked. Then they cut, hammered, sanded, painted, and did everything else by hand.

When you combine this with the fact that people in Jesus' day walked everywhere they went, it seems logical to conclude that Jesus was in pretty good physical shape — probably in better condition that most of His followers today. Today we live in different times. We sit at desks for our work most days. We don't do a lot of physical labor. We don't walk as much. Now we drive wherever we need to go. We get far less physical exercise than the men of Jesus' day.

Modern conveniences are great, but they can blind us to an essential truth: we were created to move. Our bodies work best when we move them. Our bodies work best when we get our heart rate up and get our blood moving within us. That's why our first recommendation for every Renegade Pastor is this: do some aerobic exercise three times per week for at least thirty minutes each time. By "aerobic" exercise, we mean exercise that gets your heart rate up to about 60 percent of its maximum.

Aerobic exercise has many benefits — too many for us to list here. And it doesn't matter how you get it. I (Nelson) like to run, while I (Richard) prefer to ride a bike or swing dance. The key is to get your heart rate up for an extended period of time. If you can't raise your heart rate for thirty minutes at first, start wherever you are. When I (Richard) exercised for the first time in many years about three years ago, I could handle only five minutes of aerobic exercise. I started there, and now I can go for an hour or more.

We know what many of you are thinking. *Thirty minutes! Where am I supposed to find a half hour out of my day for exercise? I am already overworked. It's just not realistic.* We know, because we have been there. We also have busy schedules. But here is the hard truth: this thirty minutes is not an option — it's a necessity. Without regular physical exercise, you are not going to last in ministry.

We look at it this way: thirty minutes of aerobic exercise, three times per week, is an investment of time that gives us even more time in return. Those minutes will add years to your ministry. And more than length, this investment of time will add depth to your ministry. You will be calmer, more focused, less stressed, and better able to handle what ministry throws at you. Physical exercise is tough at first, but it gives back much more than we invest in it.

We believe, based on our experience and our reading, that physical exercise is the cornerstone of having good health — the kind of health that leads to long, fruitful ministry. It is so important that we don't think you can be a healthy Renegade Pastor unless you are engaged in regular aerobic exercise. It is the first key to becoming healthy and being able to handle ministry stress.

THE SECOND KEY: NUTRITION

The second key, which is also vital, is nutrition. What we put in our bodies in large part determines how our bodies react. When we give our bodies good, healthy food in the right amounts, we will have the energy and focus we need to keep going. When we fill our bodies with junk, we will eventually get junk in return!

We don't have the space here to give you a full treatment on what you should be eating. I (Nelson) would encourage you to pick up the book *The Healthy Renegade Pastor*, which I co-authored with Pastor Steve Reynolds, for a more detailed explanation of what we should eat and why. In this more limited space, we want to focus on two important areas: calorie control, and the amount of fat and sugar we consume.

Count Those Calories

Most Americans have no idea how much food they consume on a daily basis. One of the reasons we are such an overweight country is simply that we eat too many calories. It is very easy to do. We eat out much more than we used to, and we serve ourselves bigger portions than ever before. Those extra calories we consume are going to show up somewhere — usually around our bellies.

How do you get those calories under control? Start by being honest about what you are eating. I (Richard) use an app on my phone to keep a journal of everything I eat. The app I use is called *My Fitness Pal*, but there are many others that do the same thing. This app logs what I eat and keeps a record of how many calories I've eaten throughout the day. When I reach my calorie limit, I am done eating for the day.

Consult with your doctor to set a reasonable calorie goal for the day. For most of us, that limit will be 1,800–2,000 calories daily. As you keep track of the foods you eat, you will learn to budget your calories more effectively to give you the maximum benefit throughout the day. Counting calories is a simple, but essential way to get your eating on track!

Watch What You Eat
In the end, calories are the most important indicator of whether you will gain weight. If you eat too much, even of good foods, you will still be overweight. But what you eat can have a huge impact on how efficiently your body reacts to you. Most Americans eat far too much fat and sugar. It is one of the things that contributes to the high obesity rates in this country.

Most prepared foods, and especially foods made for us in restaurants, are high in fat and sugar. That is bad news for many of us pastors, because we are notorious for eating meals on the road. And these high-fat, high-sugar, high-calorie foods don't only make us fat. They make us sluggish. They make our thinking foggy and slow.

How can you overcome the effects of these types of foods? Replace them with foods that are good for you! Eat more natural foods, more fruits and vegetables. Take healthy snacks with you. Switching to a fruit and vegetable–based diet will make a huge difference in your level of health.

THE BOTTOM LINE FOR GOOD HEALTH

Obviously, there is a lot more we could say about healthy living. It's something that is easy to overlook, especially when you are young. But the sooner you decide to live a healthy life, the better off you will be and the more effective your ministry will be!

All the books you can read about healthy living boil down to two essential keys: exercise and a healthy diet. If you decide that you will make these two things part of your life, you are far more likely to have a longer, more fruitful, less taxing ministry. And the rest of our lives will benefit also! Here are the keys in a nutshell:

- *Get aerobic exercise three days a week for at least thirty minutes per day. Aerobic* means that your heart rate gets up to at least 60 percent of its maximum. If you can't do that at the beginning, do as much as you can safely, and work your way up to it.

- *Count your calories!* Many Americans consume far more calories than they think. And those calories will end up becoming extra weight for you. Keep track of everything you eat, and once you hit your calorie limit for the day, stop eating.

- *Cut down on high-fat, high-sugar, high-calorie foods.* These foods will slow you down, in more ways than one. Instead, think healthy, fresh foods that will fuel your body for the work you give it to do!

Doing these things isn't just important for your physical health. It's really a spiritual endeavor. It's one way of saying to God, "Thank you for this body you have given me. I'm going to take care of it the best way I know how!" In return, you get a healthier body, better ability to handle stress, more energy and passion, and a longer, more fruitful life.

Chapter 7

DECOMPRESS EVERY DAY

*Don't worry about tomorrow, because tomorrow will worry about itself.
Each day has enough trouble of its own.*
— MATTHEW 6:34

Pastor Alex Average would describe himself as a passionate leader. He cares about what he is doing. Some might even say that he cares too much. Pastor Alex has been known to conduct himself in a way that some would describe as very unbecoming a pastor. Specifically, he sometimes snaps at people (verbally, of course). He is angry sometimes, and he has trouble hiding it. It isn't accurate to say that he doesn't love his staff or his congregation. He loves them fiercely. But his frustration sometimes overwhelms him.

In fact, *overwhelmed* is a great word to use to describe how Pastor Alex often feels. The pressure of ministry sometimes overwhelms him to the point that it boils over and affects other people. Often the daily stresses of ministry just get the best of him. He can't, or won't, let those stresses go. So he pays the price in fractured relationships and frequent turnover in his staff. People who work with him love him, but the work atmosphere is less than pleasant.

Of course, the stress and frustration also carries over into Pastor Alex's family life. He finds himself being irritable with his wife and kids, even though they haven't done anything to deserve it. The real source for his frustration is someone he dealt with while he was at work. But his family pays the price. He knows this isn't fair, and he wishes he could do things differently. But he has trouble letting go of the things that stress him out.

Pastor Rob Renegade is also a passionate minister who loves what he does. And he is no less frustrated with parts of his job than Pastor Alex is. After all, stress is a regular part of ministry. But he has learned a valuable secret: he doesn't need to carry his frustrations with him throughout his day. He chooses to let those frustrations go as the day progresses. He has developed specific strategies that help him do just that. His staff appreciates his peaceful demeanor, knowing that they won't receive his anger just because they were at the wrong place at the wrong time. As a result, staff members tend to stick around.

Pastor Rob's family also appreciates his decision to let frustrations go. They know that he is not going to lash out at them for things they didn't do. He finds that his home life is much more peaceful since he decided to decompress from daily ministry stress before he gets home. They get the best of him, not just leftovers! Pastor Rob is able to have a happy, satisfying, balanced life, because he realizes that although stress is constant, he can deal with it effectively.

THE MINUTE-BY-MINUTE BATTLE AGAINST STRESS

We don't need to tell you that being a pastor is a demanding occupation. (After all, that's the reason you have this book!) We need to keep in mind that our stress levels can rise every minute of the day. If we aren't careful, we can find ourselves continually building pressure until we are ready to explode.

The reason this happens is that we don't let stresses go. We hold onto them until we can't hold any more. When the stress gets to be too much to bear, we tend to see it by how we react in other taxing situations. Do you see yourself in any of the following reactions to stress?

- *You shut down emotionally.* When our stress level gets too high, we often find ourselves not able to invest emotionally in our environment. After all, we can stretch ourselves only to a certain point. If we are still fighting previous battles or ruminating on previous encounters, we won't have emotions left to engage the current circumstances.

- *You disengage from people.* When we are overly stressed, we tend to shy away from those things that stress us out. And that includes people. The problem is, we are in the people business. We can't do our job effectively if we are avoiding people. And we also can't do our job effectively if we are constantly angry or frustrated. Stress causes us to be less effective leaders and ministers.

- *You get overly angry about relatively minor events.* When our stress level is high, we lose the ability to respond appropriately to frustrating issues. While most of us will never explode into violence or yell at co-workers or other ministers, we can respond with a level of anger that isn't warranted. And that means we can make circumstances worse instead of better. We also run the risk of hurting people by being overly angry.

- *You become physically fatigued.* Stress is not only emotionally and mentally taxing, it can cause us to become physically exhausted. If we don't do things to release our stress during the day, we will be overwhelmed. And that will affect us physically. We won't just be more tired. We will also likely be overweight and have all the health effects that come with it. Decompressing isn't just a good idea — it's a necessity!

Many of us haven't really thought about the effects of stress on our minds and bodies. And most pastors have never thought about how we can minimize the effects of stress. This may be new territory for you. But it is vitally important, so we want to give you several strategies that will help you learn to decompress on a daily basis.

Since these may be new for you, let us give you a word of warning: you will need to really think about how you can implement these strategies, at least at the beginning. That means it may slow you down a bit. But we can assure you, from personal experience, that when you implement these strategies, you will see the difference in your health, your ministry, and your family. Eventually, many of these strategies will become second nature to you. And you will continue to reap the benefits of doing these things. So stay with it, even if it feels like you are going slowly at first.

Strategy #1: Alternate High-Stress and Low-Stress Activities

If we really examine the activities of our day, we are sure to see that not all our activities are taxing. Some are enjoyable; others, we may find inconsequential or at least tolerable. It is a good idea to intersperse low-stress activities among those things that we do find stressful. That way we have a chance to breathe and relax before we go back into high-stress contexts.

Strategy #2: Remember to Leave Your Stress at the Last Meeting

Let's face it — some meetings are VERY stressful. Maybe you are having a conflict with another staff member. Or maybe you have a volunteer with a less-than-stellar attitude. The key here is to remember to leave your feelings of anger and frustration at your last meeting. You might want to consciously put those feelings in an imaginary bucket or trash can. Be intentional about leaving your stress — and do not go back later to pick it up.

Strategy #3: Use Transition Times to Reduce Stress

There will be days when you have literally no time between demanding appointments. But even on those days, you have times of transition between activities. Make sure you use those transitions effectively to decompress. Later in this chapter, we will have some specific tips for decompressing. For now, just be intentional about using your transition times as times to get rid of stress.

Strategy #4: Decompress before You Go Home

This is probably the most important of all the strategies we give you. As bad as it is to carry stress between activities at work, it is far worse to carry it home to affect your family. This is a sure path to family conflict, and it is almost entirely avoidable. Make the commitment between you and God that you will not take out your frustrations on your spouse and kids. They deserve better from you; be sure you give it to them.

Once you see these areas where you have the opportunity (even the responsibility) to decompress, you still must actually do it. And that can be difficult, especially if you are accustomed to holding on to your stress and frustrations. In the next section, we will give you specific activities you can engage in to decompress from even the most overwhelming day. The more of these strategies that you employ, the better you will be able to handle stress.

TIPS FOR DECOMPRESSING EFFECTIVELY

Certain activities are proven stress reducers. Some will no doubt be familiar to you; others may be new. Try them all, and use the ones you find to be most effective.

Tip #1: Write Down Your Stress

I (Richard) read a book many years ago that I believe was entitled *Strictly Personal and Confidential: The Letters Harry Truman Never Mailed.* Apparently, the former president had a habit of calling in his secretary to dictate angry letters to reporters, congressmen, and even cabinet members who had said or done something to frustrate or anger him. He would dictate these letters — and he didn't hold back. The letters were sarcastic, frequently hilarious — and probably would have done great damage to Truman's presidency had he sent them.

But Truman never sent them. Instead, he would tell his secretary to put the letter in her desk and keep it there. A day or two later, Truman would come back to the letter and think better of sending it. He would compose another, less angry letter instead. Writing that initial letter was Truman's way of blowing off steam without anyone being harmed.

We can learn a lot from the practice of this former president. Writing things down is a great way to let our frustrations out. And as long as we don't send those letters (or emails, or texts), no one will be harmed. This idea works well, no matter whether our writings take the form of letters or a personal journal. In fact, Christians throughout history have written about their joys and frustrations in journals.

Allow us to give you a couple of hints about keeping a journal that will help you get your frustrations out more effectively:

- *Be as honest as you can be.* Since this isn't for anyone else to read, you don't have to worry about being polite or phrasing everything correctly. Instead, just say what you are feeling in the moment. No one else needs to know.

- *Keep your journal secure.* Since you are writing things that are private and could potentially be hurtful to others, you need to keep it secure. Store it in a locked drawer.

If you are writing on a tablet or computer, keep that file protected with a password. Make sure others can't read these private thoughts.

Tip #2: Cry Out to God

We love reading all of God's Word, but the Psalms are especially precious to us. These are the songs of the Jewish people, and they cover the whole range of human emotions — joy, sadness, anger, frustration. Many of these Psalms are simply prayers in which the psalmist cries out to God about what is on his heart.

It's amazing to read how many of the Psalms express a deep level of frustration and anger, much of it directed at God Himself! We often see phrases like, "God, why are you so far away?" and "Lord, why do you allow the wicked to prosper, while righteous people go hungry?" And the truly amazing thing is, God doesn't appear to mind. He can handle our anger, our frustration, our lack of understanding.

Sometimes we mistakenly think that we shouldn't bring our negative emotions to God. But the truth is, we should take everything to Him, including our frustrations in life and ministry. He is more than able to handle anything we can throw at Him. In fact, He is the only one who can actually do anything to fix the problems we face.

Don't hesitate to bring your anger, stress, and frustrations to God. Let Him work in you and in the ones causing the problem. Turn to His Word to find peace, and maybe insight into the issues you are facing.

We are going to give you the same warnings here as we did when we discussed keeping a journal. The first is, be honest when you pray. If the Psalms teach us anything, it is that we don't need to hide anything from Him. So let Him know exactly what is on your mind.

The second is this: If you write your prayers down, make sure you keep them secure. Other people might mistake your honesty with God for a lack of faith, or something else. Lock it away, or keep it protected in some way.

Tip #3: Change Your Way of Thinking

Research has shown us repeatedly that one thing is true: how we think about a situation determines how we react to it. We need to rethink the way we see the frustrating episodes in our ministry. Once we start to think about them differently, our stress level will often drop. That makes it easier for us to leave it behind at work.

First, begin thinking of the stresses you face as God-given opportunities to grow. If you really believe that God works all things for your good, then there must be a purpose in everything He allows. That doesn't make everything that happens good. But it does mean there is something worthwhile in every demanding situation. You need to look for what God is trying to teach you.

Second, begin thinking of frustrating circumstances as challenges. Frustrations just sit there and bother us. Challenges are something that can be attacked and overcome. What if every stressful episode is really a challenge that you need to overcome? That makes you an active participant in finding the solution to every exasperating challenge.

We readily acknowledge that it takes time and energy to change your thinking. It does not happen overnight. But with time and intentionality, you can begin to see things differently. Changing your way of thinking won't change the situation. But it does change your response to it. It redefines how you see what's happening around you. With a new perspective on your stressors, you might even see novel solutions that weren't apparent before. At the very least, it will lower your stress level and make it easier to decompress.

Tip #4: Keep a Positive, Thankful Outlook

As pastors, we can't allow negative, anxious thoughts to overwhelm us — at least not for long. After all, we serve a big, amazing God who is greater than all our troubles. When we focus on everything that's wrong around us, we can become defeated. But if we keep our focus on the things that are going right, we might just see the victory ahead.

Staying focused on the positive isn't being a Pollyanna. It's based in the fact of who God is and His love for us. If the Creator of the universe is on my side, working out everything for my good, then I know that even the worst frustrations can't last forever. He may require me to make some changes to resolve an issue. He may ask me to do some things that are uncomfortable in order to make a breakthrough. But I can decompress better when I realize that God is looking out for me.

And, isn't this a great testimony for us to give to our church? It increases the faith of those we pastor when they can see that we seek after God even when things look dark. After all, those in our churches are going through some sort of struggles. We can help them get through by keeping our focus on what God is doing in the big picture, not on our present circumstances.

That is the essence of what faith is — trusting God to bring something good out of a bad, frustrating, taxing circumstance. If He really is as trustworthy as we say He is, then we need to look to Him no matter what is going on around us.

Tip #5: Change Your Behavior

If you are going to decompress effectively from a stressful day (or any challenging event during the day), you will need to change your behavior. Some of those changes are obvious: keeping a journal, as we discussed earlier; praying honestly about what's going on; and making a change in your thinking about stressful circumstances. But there is more than that. You will need to adopt some different actions in order to decompress:

- *Make exercise a part of your daily routine.* We talked about the benefits of exercise in the last chapter, so we won't cover it in detail here. But you need to make exercise a regular part of your day. It's a great way to relieve stress before you get home. Another time to get in some exercise is during the transition times we talked about earlier in this chapter. You may not have long, but even a ten-minute walk is enough to get your heart pumping and to clear out some tension-filled thoughts and emotions.

- *Do something to get your mind off stress.* That can include any of the strategies we gave you earlier in this chapter, or it could be something simple like reading or listening to relaxing music. Anything you can do that gets your mind away from the things that are frustrating you.

Of course, you can't avoid your stressors forever. You must face them at some point. But having just a few minutes away can give you the renewed energy and focus you need to tackle the problems you are facing. Take a few minutes to distract yourself, then return to fight the battle at hand.

Tip #6: Remember You Can Fight Only One Day at a Time

We hope you noticed the verse we quoted at the beginning of this chapter. In it, Jesus encourages His followers not to worry about the future. He says, "Each day has enough trouble of its own." In other words, you can fight against stress and frustrations only one day at a time. Tomorrow will have a whole new set of stressors and frustrations.

We like to think we know what's going to happen in the future. But in reality, we don't know what's coming. A problem we thought was going to crush us might come to nothing, while something we never considered attacks us from behind. But we will never win playing the what-if game. We waste a lot energy deciding how we are going to fight a battle that may never come our way.

Another problem with trying to fight future battles today is that we tend to make things that are unknown bigger and scarier than they actually are. We may believe we will fight a giant monster tomorrow, when in reality, we will just need to swat away a few moths. Don't waste energy, time, and focus fighting a bigger enemy that doesn't really exist.

Instead, focus all your energy on the battles at hand. Take the word of Jesus seriously, and leave tomorrow's worries in the future.

LET IT GO!

If we don't develop the habit of decompressing after every stressful day, and even during each day, we will carry that stress with us everywhere. And the effects will devastate our ministries and our family lives.

In order to decompress effectively, take these opportunities to decompress during each day:

- *Alternate between high-stress and low-stress activities.* Whenever possible, schedule activities you enjoy in between those that cause you stress.

- *Leave the stress from your last meeting at your last meeting.* Visualize yourself leaving your stress, like a package, at the site of your last meeting. And don't bother to pick it up again.

- *Use the natural transition times during the day to decompress.* Take advantage of the natural breaks in the day to do some of things we recommend to let go of stress.

- *Be sure to decompress before you go home to your family.* This is the most important time to decompress. The time you spend with your family is sacred — don't ruin it with the stresses of the day!

Those are the natural times during the day when you can let go of the stress that has accumulated. Now remember these tips that will help you decompress effectively:

- *Write down your stresses and frustrations in a journal.*

- *Pray honestly, passionately, even angrily to God about the things that are stressing you out.*

- *Change your way of thinking.* Try to find what God is trying to teach you in every difficult circumstance. Think of your stressors as challenges that can be overcome.

- *Approach every concern with an attitude of positivity and gratitude.* No matter how large your troubles, God is always bigger.

- *Make changes in your behavior.* Exercise to get your frustrations out. Get your mind off your present stressors. Decide to take action against your stress.

- *Remember to leave tomorrow's troubles for tomorrow.* You can fight only one day at a time. You will only drain your time, energy, and focus if you try to fight tomorrow's battles today.

Keep these tips in mind as you face each new day. Make the commitment to let stress go so that it doesn't weigh you down and steal your joy. Ministry is never easy. But if we learn to let go of stress, we can keep that stress from robbing us of the joy God desires for us.

Chapter 8

TALK TO THE RIGHT PEOPLE ABOUT YOUR STRESS

There is a friend who stays closer than a brother.
PROVERBS 18:24

Loneliness is an affliction that affects many pastors. Pastor Alex Average is one of them. He is reluctant to let people — especially people in his church — get too close to him. He fears being hurt or disappointed by them on a personal level. He doesn't have close friends outside of his church either. He is extremely busy, and he uses his busyness as an excuse to not make friends. But he also finds that many people outside vocational ministry have trouble relating to what he's going through. And other pastors that he might befriend are just as busy as he is.

Pastor Alex is good at making polite conversation. But he rarely talks deeply about the joys, disappointments, and frustrations of ministry. As a result, he carries much of the stress of ministry within himself, with no outlet. Sometimes, Alex just wants to have a "normal" job, one where it would be easier to connect with other people. But God called him to ministry, so he goes on — alone.

Pastor Rob Renegade also knows loneliness. There are times when it feels overwhelming. But Pastor Rob has taken the words of Scripture seriously and has friends in whom he can confide. It's not a big group, but these men love Rob and are ready to talk with him about the things that are most important to him.

Pastor Rob has one friend in particular whom he has known for many years. He has experience in pastoral ministry. Most importantly, this man is a strong Christian who has a great deal of wisdom. He listens to Rob and helps him see his challenges from a different perspective. Just having someone who listens to him is great comfort for Pastor Rob. Having someone who is wise enough to help him work through issues is an even greater blessing.

Most of the people in Pastor Rob's church have no idea that he has this support system. After all, none of these friends are very prominent in his church. What they do see is a more relaxed pastor, one who can help them because he isn't overly burdened with his own cares. They see a pastor who can recognize the different sides of issues that come up. He often realizes solutions that escape others, simply because his perspective is broader. They sincerely appreciate the wisdom Pastor Rob brings to their challenges. They may not fully understand it, but the members of his congregation should be extremely thankful for the friends and advisors that Rob surrounds himself with. They are a large part of the success of his ministry.

LONELINESS IS A MINISTRY KILLER

There is little doubt that loneliness is one of the biggest problems facing pastors today. Every survey reports that most pastors experience this emotion, often on a regular basis. This may sound strange to many people. After all, aren't we pastors surrounded by people for large portions of our ministry? We lead groups, we preach, we meet with staff and volunteers. How could we possibly be lonely?

The answer is simple: When we experience loneliness, what we are really missing is a connection. We are missing fulfillment of the universal human need to have close relationships with other people. God created us for community. In the Garden of Eden, God looked at Adam and said, "It isn't good for man to be alone" (Gen. 2:18). This is still very true today.

But ministry can be a very lonely calling for us. People come to us with challenging issues that are also deeply personal. They naturally expect a high level of privacy, and we give it to them. Our job is so specialized and different from other occupations that there aren't many people who even understand what we deal with on a daily and weekly basis. I (Richard) once had a church member who seriously thought I worked only one hour per week — Sunday morning! He was shocked when I corrected his perception of my job.

Not only do we have a job that some people find it hard to relate to, we also suffer because we are so busy. It takes time to develop relationships, and time is something we don't have a lot of. Many of us come to the conclusion that making close friendships just isn't worth the effort. As a result, we suffer the consequences of loneliness.

THE CONSEQUENCES OF LONELINESS

Loneliness has a high cost attached to it. It takes an emotional and physical toll on us. And the consequences get worse as the years go on. These are just a few of the effects of loneliness:

- *Pastors who are lonely are less healthy.* There is a correlation between health and having a strong support system. People with friends tend to eat better, exercise more, and take better care of themselves. One study even found that doctors said they give better medical care to those with a solid support system.

- *Pastors who are lonely are more depressed.* This is probably the natural result of not having close companions to share life with. In the general population, loneliness is a key factor in many suicides. Since we were created for community, we find it harder to be happy when we are alone.

- *Pastors who are lonely have less satisfaction in their lives.* Again, this probably stems from the fact that we enjoy life more when we share it with someone else. Our joy seems to be tied to our ability to share things with people who are close to us.

- *Pastors who are lonely create more stress hormones in their bodies.* We pay a physical price for being lonely. These stress hormones cause us to put on weight and get less sleep, as well as having all kinds of other negative effects on our bodies.

- *Pastors who are lonely get less sleep, and their sleep is less effective.* The stress hormones also cause our sleep to be less restorative, so we don't get the full benefit of sleep when we are lonely.

All of these are cumulative, meaning that they get worse over time. Loneliness extracts a high price from those it afflicts. As a pastor, you can't afford to pay that price. And as a Renegade Pastor, the good news is you don't need to. In this chapter, we will give you some important traits to look for in a good friend. That should make the process easier. Right now, we just want to encourage you, because having a friend you can confide in is not an idea we came up with. It was God's idea first.

WHAT GOD SAYS ABOUT CLOSE RELATIONSHIPS

As we said earlier, God created us to have close relationships. When we don't have these close relationships, we are actually living out of step with the way God created us.

The great people of God had companions, almost without exception. (The ones who didn't often found themselves in trouble.) We could start with Adam and Eve. Moses had Aaron as his companion. The kings had their advisors. (Granted, some of them weren't very good.) In the New Testament, Jesus had the twelve disciples. When He sent out messengers to the cities where He was going, He sent them out in pairs. Paul always traveled with several companions, including Barnabas, Silas, Timothy, and others. There is a definite pattern in Scripture of people doing ministry together.

Let's consider some verses that relate to this idea that friends are a necessity if we want to live the life God has created for us:

"And if someone overpowers one person, two can resist him. A cord of three strands is not easily broken." — Ecclesiastes 4:12
There is a level of strength that comes from having friends who are looking out for you. Notice that it's a cord of three strands, not ten or twelve. You don't need an army of close friends. Just a couple of close friends can be your army.

"A fool's way is right in his own eyes, but whoever listens to counsel is wise." — Proverbs 12:15
Later in this chapter, we will examine one of the most important aspects of having close friendships: getting a fresh perspective. We normally see things from our own limited perspective. When we have friends surrounding us, though, we can take advantage of their expanded perspective.

> *"Listen to counsel and receive instruction so that you may be wise later in life."* — Proverbs 19:20

> And *"Finalize plans with counsel, and wage war with sound guidance."* — Proverbs 20:18
> Most pastors we know are quite wise, able to discern problems and their solutions. When you have friends who are also wise, you just multiply the wisdom that is available to you. And we don't know any pastor who doesn't need additional wisdom in their lives.

> *"A friend loves at all times, and a brother is born for a difficult time."* — Proverbs 17:17
> We always need friends around us. But we feel that need for friendship the most when we are going through difficult times. When things are darkest for us, we need friends who will be a light for us. Otherwise, the darkness can be overwhelming.

The Bible has much to say about friendship; we had a chance to scratch only the surface here. But it should be clear that God wants us to have people close to us. People who are our partners, even if they aren't in ministry themselves. God does not want us to go through life alone. It's a miserable way to live, because friendships add so much to our lives. And going it alone robs us of the chance for people to bless us and for us to be a blessing to others.

We firmly believe that you won't have the kind of ministry God wants you to have unless you have at least one friend whom you can confide in and get wisdom and guidance from. That may sound like a strong statement, but we have seen it too many times. Pastors get locked in an ivory tower, apart from their congregations and everyone else. Perhaps for a while they can get by on their natural abilities and God-given gifts. But eventually, their ministry suffers.

It may not be noticeable at first, but at some point, everyone will see the deficiencies.

We mention this concept from time to time, and we will do it again here: when you follow the commands of Scripture to have close friends in your life, you are not just doing something that benefits you; it will also benefit your congregation. Whether we are conscious of it or not, we are role models and examples for our congregations. People follow what we do, even more than what we say. We need to have close friends whom we trust and confide in, so that our church members see how important it is. Then they will do it in their own lives as well.

GAIN ANOTHER PERSPECTIVE

In my (Nelson's) coaching networks, I talk about the value of G — A — P. That stands for Gain Another Perspective. It is one of the most important reasons why we need people who are close to us and can speak wisdom into our lives. A close friend can see things in our lives and circumstances that may be hidden from us.

Are they hidden because we are not smart enough to see them? Not at all. As we said earlier, pastors are some of the brightest, most perceptive people we know. But we are all limited. We are shaped to see things a certain way by our temperament, our experiences, our upbringing, our education, and many other things. We can't notice everything. We often miss critical details that would otherwise affect our decisions.

Also keep in mind that it is sometimes difficult to make good decisions when we are in the middle of a tough circumstance. Our emotions get involved, and we are no longer thinking clearly. I'm sure most of us have said or done things out of anger or frustration that we later wish we hadn't said or done. Someone who is close to us can help us see things clearly because they don't have the same level of emotional involvement.

This is one reason why both of us are so passionate about the value of coaching. I (Nelson) have been coaching pastors for a number of years. In addition to the instruction I offer in church systems, church health, and living as a Renegade Pastor, I often serve as an extra pair of eyes for pastors who are facing tough conditions. It's actually a great privilege for me to come alongside these fellow ministers and help them in any way I can. (By the way, if you would like to learn more about my coaching networks, and how to partner with me to grow yourself and your church, just go to www.RenegadeStressManagement.com. It is an investment in your ministry that you will not regret.)

Coaching can be an invaluable tool in your growth as a pastor and as a person. We highly recommend you find a caring, experienced leader who will walk alongside you on this journey. A coach should have a wealth of experience that gives you a fresh perspective on your situation.

We also suggest that you should have at least one friend, someone you know personally, who can give you an additional perspective on your circumstances. It doesn't need to be another pastor, although sometimes that is helpful. But it should be someone with wisdom who will speak candidly about what they see in any given instance. If you have someone like this in your life, they will be more valuable to you than gold.

And, of course, if you have such a person speaking into your life, you need to be humble enough to receive their words, even if they aren't pleasant. You may not want to hear what they have to say. But you may *need* to hear what they have to say, and act on it. This is an important component of having someone give you another perspective — you must be willing to do something! If you don't change based on what this person tells you, there is no reason for them to talk to you.

THE NECESSARY QUALITIES OF A CLOSE FRIEND

What does this person, who is a friend, an advisor, and a confidant, look like? Are there certain qualities that make a person fit for this position in your life? These are important questions, because for many average pastors, they have never had someone like this in their lives. You may feel fearful of having someone who has that kind of power in your life. How do you know you can trust them?

When I (Richard) first came to the church I now serve, there was quite a bit of division within the congregation. Two factions were at war with each other, and it wasn't pretty! One thing I knew, if I became close friends with anyone who was involved in the conflict, I would likely get bad advice from them. Even if they meant well, too much bad blood existed on both sides for me to be able to trust the advice I might receive. Although I became close with many of the people who were there at the time, I took my wisdom and advice from friends outside the church.

That may not be true for you in your ministry. It's likely that there is someone in your church who would give you great counsel, if you allow it. But you should know what to look for in someone who will be that "friend who sticks closer than a brother":

- *This person should be a follower of Jesus.* We are not saying that only Christians can display wisdom, or that you can't find counsel in secular sources. But we believe that the people who are closest to you, the ones who are speaking into your life, should be followers of Jesus.

  Why is this important? You want someone talking to you who shares your values and your way of looking at the world. Otherwise, at some point there will likely be a conflict as your friend's worldview clashes with your own.

- *This person should be actively growing in his/her faith.* It isn't enough that a confidant is a follower of Jesus. He or she needs to be serious about his/her faith. They need to be actively seeking Jesus, growing in the important areas of life.

  How do you know if someone is serious about their faith? It isn't someone who carries the largest Bible or talks the most about their faith. Instead look for someone who looks like Jesus in their thoughts and behavior. If they are loving, kind, servant-hearted, gentle, and so forth, that person might be a good choice.

- *This person should demonstrate wisdom in other areas of his/her life.* You want someone who has demonstrated a level of wisdom in other areas, so he/she can bring that wisdom into play in your life. Look at several key areas: How do they treat their spouse? Does their marriage appear to be going well? How do they relate to their kids? Are they loving and kind toward other people? Do they serve willingly?

  If you can, look into how they are regarded at work. Are they highly thought of? Do they work hard? All these things can give you insight into how they will be as a close friend/advisor.

- *This person should demonstrate faithfulness in other areas.* This goes to the heart of the concern many pastors have about having a close confidant: Will this person keep our conversations and my secrets safe? We are big believers that the words of Jesus should inform us in this area: "Whoever is faithful in very little is also faithful in much, and whoever is unrighteous in very little is also

unrighteous in much" (Luke 16:10). Don't trust someone with big things until you see they are faithful in
smaller things.

- *If possible, choose someone who knows you well.* This isn't
always possible, especially if you haven't taken time in
recent years to cultivate close relationships. But there is
a comfort in knowing people for long periods of time.
That isn't to say that people you have known for shorter
periods can't become important to you.

  People who have known you for a while know your
idiosyncrasies. They probably have shared experiences
with you. Importantly, they know your weak spots, and
might know where your blind spots are. If you have a
close friend you've known from childhood or a dorm-
mate from college, that is a blessing you should cherish.

When you find a person who fulfills these qualifications, you have
probably found someone who can be a good friend for you. Take the
time to develop a richer, deeper relationship with this person. Don't
be afraid to open your heart and soul to this person.

It might also be a good idea to tell this person that you are looking
for someone you can depend on, someone you can confide in. Most
people understand the human need to connect deeply with others.
They have probably felt a similar need in their own life. Honesty is
the basis for any deep relationship, so don't be afraid to be honest.

What if you find someone who has all the qualities you are looking for, yet the two of you don't connect? It's not a big deal. Simply
count this person as a friend who doesn't quite measure up to the
standard you set for a confidant. Then move on to another candi-
date. He or she is out there!

WE NEED CLOSE RELATIONSHIPS

We hope that you have discovered in this chapter that you need close friends who can help you handle difficulties, give you a needed alternate perspective, and add to your ministry's effectiveness. Renegade Pastors know that you can't do this alone. You desperately need other people.

We should also not discount the fact that God's Word is clear that we need to have people in our lives who help us, encourage us, and make us wiser, better people. We should never discount the examples, from Moses to Paul, of people working in teams. If it was necessary for those servants of God, who are we to ignore its effectiveness now? God's people, working together, can accomplish great things.

Remember also the necessary qualities you want to see in someone who is going to fulfill this role in your life. This person should:

- *Be a follower of Jesus.* Pick someone who is saved. This person should share your worldview and values, which will keep you from having complications later on. While you can find wisdom from unbelievers, your closest advisors need to be Christians.

- *Be committed to growing in Christian maturity.* You want someone who is becoming more like Jesus in every way. With that maturity comes the wisdom and discernment that you will rely on when you are facing tough times. Don't just go for someone who talks about Jesus. You need to see a Christian lifestyle!

- *Demonstrate wisdom in different areas of their lives.* People with wisdom show that wisdom in many areas of their lives, not just in ministry. So look at their marriage, their workplace, how they treat people around the church. Ask yourself: do they demonstrate wisdom in these areas?

- *Demonstrate faithfulness in different areas.* Can this person keep a secret or hold things in confidence? Many people struggle in this area. You need someone who can be trusted to keep important things confidential.

- *Be someone you've known for a while, if possible.* This isn't always a possibility. But never discount the joy and comfort of someone you have known for a while. Cultivate those long-lasting relationships!

Friends and confidants are essential for any Renegade Pastor. Yes, it takes time and effort to develop friendships. But the rewards of doing so far outweigh the cost! Don't allow loneliness to rob your ministry. Instead, seek out the company, wisdom, and joy that comes from close, lasting friendships.

Chapter 9

PRAISE GOD THROUGH THE STRESS

Let all who take refuge in you rejoice; let them shout for joy forever.
— PSALM 5:11

Pastor Alex Average is finding it difficult to handle his current level of stress. His faith is strong — he still loves Jesus just as much as he always has. But he also knows that if he doesn't find a way to lower his stress level, he will need to find another occupation. It's just taking too big a toll on him emotionally, physically, mentally, and spiritually. He loves being in ministry. He just doesn't know why it needs to be so hard.

Pastor Rob Renegade takes a very different approach to ministry stress. He is intimately familiar with the pressures of pastoring a local church. But Pastor Rob is different from Pastor Alex in at least one major way: he makes praise a huge part of his stress-management strategy. He has learned that praise is the "secret weapon" that keeps him sane when stress is closing in around him.

Pastor Rob does several things that keep him in a worshipful spirit all day long. He keeps a journal of all the prayers God has answered for him. When he reads it, he is often brought to tears thinking of

God's mercy and provision. He remembers that God has a plan in every circumstance. God is always working, even if Rob can't see what He has in mind. This one thought reminds him that God is in control and that He will accomplish His purposes in Rob's ministry.

Rob is careful to include praise in his personal prayer life. He, like many of us, finds it very easy to spend all of his prayer time asking God for things or just complaining about his present circumstances. Because he sets aside time for praise, Rob finds that he is able to keep his problems in perspective. It may feel like everything is spinning out of control sometimes. But the reality is that God is always bigger than his problems. That gives Rob great comfort.

Pastor Rob Renegade finds that the peace he receives when he is praising God spills over into different areas of his ministry. He is able to remain joyful, even in the midst of difficult times, because he stays focused on the One who ultimately controls his destiny.

PRAISE: THE NEGLECTED WEAPON AGAINST STRESS

At first, praise may not sound like a powerful way to overcome stress. But in this chapter, we will talk about why it works and give you some practical tips that will help you become a person who praises first — and stresses later!

We believe there are at least a couple of reasons why we don't think of praise as an effective strategy against ministry stress. The first is simply that as pastors, we are usually people of action. We want to be doing something. It's easy for us to fail to see praise as an action step that we need to take. After all, when you are praising God, you may feel like you aren't doing anything about the problem. You aren't having tough conversations. You aren't working on the broken or missing systems in your church. You aren't developing staff or volunteers. From this perspective, it can look very much as though praising God is a way to avoid dealing with stress.

Let us urge you that this is not the case. The benefits you get from praising God make it an essential weapon in the fight against stress. In fact, you won't win the stress battle without it.

The second reason we believe many pastors neglect to use worship as part of their stress management strategies is that it appears counterintuitive in many ways. Stress is, by its nature, unpleasant — even painful. No one seeks out stress! But praise is just the opposite. It is good. It makes us feel good. We praise God for His blessings, for His provisions. How can we praise Him for something like stress?

But praise and worship is an important part of handling stress. Pastors who choose to praise God, even in the midst of their stress, are pastors who will last. You cannot neglect this God-given weapon that will help you handle stress more effectively.

THE NEGATIVE EFFECTS OF LOSING FOCUS

The truth is that the only way you can handle the stress of ministry effectively is by remembering to praise God in the middle of it. There is no way around it. We are created to worship, no matter who we are. Before we become followers of Jesus, we worship all kinds of false gods. Some of us worship money. Others worship power or sex. Some of us worship sports. Every human being worships something.

When we become followers of Jesus, the focus of our praise and worship changes. We recognize that God alone is worthy of our praise. And, if we neglect that praise, we find that we are missing out on some important things. When we forget to praise God in the midst of our stress, we miss out on a lot of necessary things, and some bad things tend to happen within us:

- *We become lonely in ministry.* We are created to have fellowship with God. That means He walks with us through all the seasons of life — not just the good times. When we neglect the weapon of praise, we are leaving God out of the picture. It's ironic that we would leave our closest friend out of our lives at the very moment we need Him the most. Yet, that's what happens when we neglect praise and worship.

Neglecting God causes us great loneliness, as you no doubt know. He is our closest and dearest friend. There is no reason to leave Him out of the difficult times.

- *We become overwhelmed by the stress of ministry.* You have probably heard the old expression, "God will never give you more than you can handle!" While we appreciate the sentiment behind the statement, we are not convinced that it's true. It's probably more accurate to say that God sometimes gives us more than we can handle so that we can learn to trust Him and depend on Him.

When we praise God, even in the middle of our stress, we are giving Him the opportunity to share in our struggles. We are, in essence, inviting Him to work in His power and provision. God never wastes an opportunity to help us grow. Praise is our way of saying, "Do what you do best, Lord!"

- *Our perception of who God is shrinks.* When we are in the middle of difficulties it is easy to forget how big, how powerful, how good God is. God never loses His strength.

Praise reminds us of who God really is. We are constantly bombarded by doubts about who God is. We need praise to balance out the negative, false messages we hear and see on a daily basis. God is bigger than our problems; we need to always remember that.

- *We forget what we have been called to do.* We have said it before, including within the pages of this book: we believe there is no more important occupation on earth than that of a local church pastor. And God has given us the privilege of working for Him in this vital position. But the stress of the position, and the problems that come with it, sometimes make us forget how important we are in God's plan.

  We need to praise God so that we see these stressors as opportunities, as speed bumps, as part of God's plan for us. Otherwise, we will be discouraged. We might even believe that God is through with us. Praise gives us the proper perspective on what's going on around us, so we can see things the way God sees them.

We can see from this list that we are truly missing out if we neglect to praise God through our trials. God intends for us to worship Him — in good times and in bad times.

WHAT WE GAIN WHEN WE PRAISE GOD THROUGH OUR STRESS

As you would expect, there are many benefits that come our way when we worship God in the middle of our stress.

This should not surprise us. God is always pleased when we turn to Him! He wants to be our constant faithful companion — a present help in our time of trouble. Let's look at some of the specific ways we benefit from praising God in the midst of our stress:

- *We get an accurate picture of how big God is and how small our stressors are.* It is really easy for our perception to get out of whack. We start to see our problems as huge, insurmountable obstacles that can never be overcome.

The reality is that God is more than able to handle whatever life (even ministry life) throws at us. He isn't surprised or overwhelmed by anything that happens. He is not only able to handle our stress, He is willing, even happy, to handle our challenges. Praise reminds us of this important fact.

- *Praising God through our stress is a great testimony to our congregations.* How do the members of our churches learn to handle tough times? We hope they are reading their Bibles. They should be praying about everything that happens in their lives. But they will learn much from watching us. We need to be good role models, showing how a believer responds to stress.

They need to see us in an attitude of praise, even when it's hard. Even when it feels like everything is falling apart around us. When we do that, they will learn how important it is for them to be grateful and thankful. God can use our stress to help our churches grow into Christlikeness.

- *Praising God through our stress brings us great peace.* The stress of ministry can become a constant source of turmoil. If we don't act on the unrest, it will soon affect every area of our lives, not just ministry. We will be in a constant state of uneasiness. Our family and friends definitely notice. This kind of stress can affect our health and wreck other aspects of our lives.

Praise brings peace. That is the simplest way to put it. When we praise God through the stress, we bring Him into the middle of it. And wherever God is, there is peace for the believer. We are reminded that we are not alone in what we are going through. We have an all-powerful, all-loving God working on our behalf.

- *Praising God through our stress renews our vision for ministry.* Most of us got into ministry because we had a clear calling from God on our lives. At the beginning, we knew exactly what God wanted us to focus on in ministry. But the daily stresses of being a pastor can make us take our eyes off the reasons why we got into ministry in the first place. Once we lose sight of our calling, we forget why we do what we do.

Praising God renews our focus on what's important. God is still in control. He still loves us, and His calling on our lives hasn't changed just because our circumstances have. I (Nelson) often tell pastors that they need to remember their calling. Praising God through our stress helps us to do just that.

THE SPECIFICS OF PRAISE

Do we need a section on how to praise God through our stress? Most of you probably say, "Come on guys. We are not just believers, saved by God's grace. We are pastors — and Renegade Pastors at that! We definitely know how to worship God." But we are including a short "Praise Primer" in this section, just as a reminder.

Why do we think you may need this section? One reason we all need a reminder is that it's in the middle of trouble when we need to be the most thankful. It's at that very moment that we need to remember how good God is. It's at that moment that we need to keep our thoughts centered on how powerful He is. It's then we need to remember that He is always working on our behalf, to do something for our good and for His glory.

But it is also at those times, when we are battered, beat up, and discouraged, that we often feel least like praising God. Remember, we are both pastors. We know exactly what it is like down in the trenches, fighting every day to lead the people of God. We know that when you're feeling weak and overwhelmed, drowning in stress, you may not feel like lifting your voice in praise. But we can tell you from experience — this is the very time you need to praise God!

So we are going to give you some gentle reminders about coming to God in praise for His provision, even in the middle of your stress. We hope you will find these keys encouraging:

- *God is pleased with the praise you bring Him, no matter what shape you're in.* You may be beaten to a pulp. You may not feel much like a Christian, let alone a pastor. But God knows what shape you're in — and He wants to hear from you. He doesn't expect us to be at our best. In fact, we believe God is most glorified when we come to Him in our weakness. As the old saying goes, "When God is all we have, we find out He is all we need."

  The key here is to make praise a regular part of your life, not something you reserve for when you feel like doing it. The more stress you feel, the less you will feel like praising God. So praise Him even when praise doesn't come easy.

- *Remember that it's okay to be angry with God — and to express that anger.* As you no doubt know, the Psalms are the songbook of the Hebrew people. As you read, you'll notice every conceivable emotion is described in these songs: joy, peace, frustration, anger. And God isn't angry with the psalmist when he expresses his frustration, or even his anger! God knows that those emotions are part of the human condition.

Be honest with God; if you are angry, tell Him. He knows it anyway. And once you have expressed your frustrations, you will be in a better place to worship Him for His goodness. Honesty with God is a great way to make sure that you don't get bitter and cynical about ministry.

- *Praise God for His work, even when you can't see what He is doing.* We often don't see what God is up to until after the storm has passed. The only thing we can rest on in those instances is the assurance that God is working out all things for our good, because we love Him (Rom. 8:28). Well, that is enough reason to praise Him. Let Him know you trust Him to work. Let Him know you are resting on His goodness and love to bring you through.

  God is good all the time. He is powerful all the time. When you decide to praise Him even when you can't see Him at work, you are acknowledging that you recognize and love Him for who He is.

Use these reminders to help you get started praising God in the middle of your stress. You are going to find that when praise is part of your life, the stresses become far more manageable. You remember that you have a big God who is always at work in your life. He will give you the insight and wisdom you need to find a way through the stress. Or, He will give you the strength to handle it for as long as it lasts.

REVIEWING THE BENEFITS OF PRAISE

This sounds almost too simple: remember to praise God in the middle of your stressful times. But we have found, and we think you will also find, that there is no more powerful weapon you can use in the battle against stress.

It is sad to us that we pastors, even good pastors, forget how important this weapon is. But if you find that you have neglected to praise God, you shouldn't beat yourself up about it. After all, you are human, frail, and sinful like the rest of us. Life comes at us like a hurricane sometimes, and it's difficult to remember the very things that will help us most. If you find that you are in this position, and you need to make praise a bigger part of your life, then simply begin where you are. Ask God to forgive you for your lack of worship, and start praising Him.

To further encourage you, remember the benefits you will see from praising God through your stress:

- *Praising God reminds us of how great God is.* It is common for us to exaggerate the size of our problems, while we underestimate God. If anything, we should reverse that trend: we need to see our problems as small and inconsequential. And we need to see God as He is — strong, powerful, and ready to act to save and protect us. That is the accurate picture of God, and it brings glory to Him.

- *Praising God gives a great example to our congregations.* Our church members struggle with the same things we do: stress, disappointments, frustrations. They need to know how to deal with it. What better role model than their pastor, who can show them the importance of praise in handling stress. You may be the only picture they see of the essential part praise holds in managing stress. Don't deprive your people of this great picture of living the Christian life.

- *Praising God brings great peace to our lives.* There is no doubt that we can all use more peace in our challenging lives. When we take time to focus on who God is and what He's doing for us, it brings us peace. And because this peace is based on God, it doesn't change with our circumstances. It really is a peace "which surpasses all understanding," as Philippians 4:7 says.

- *Praising God gives us a renewed focus on our calling.* We get stuck easily in the mud of ministry stress and frustration. But God called us for a specific purpose: to lead His people. When we praise God, we remember our calling. We focus on the big picture of what He's doing. And there is little doubt we will find renewed focus, excitement, and passion for the ministry God has called us to!

With all these benefits to praise, we hope your response as a Renegade Pastor will be to immediately begin worshiping God and continue to worship Him, no matter what storms you are enduring. We will always have stress in ministry. You cannot do anything to change that. But remember that when you praise God, you are inviting Him to show His power and love for you.

THREE QUICK REMINDERS

As you begin (or restart) this journey of praise, keep these three simple things in mind:

First, remember that you don't need to be at your best in order to bring praises to God. He is glorified when we come to Him at our lowest point, when we are battered and beaten up. He is glorified when we can say, "If need be, I will praise Him with my last breath!" In fact, it's in our weakness that we see God working in His strength.

Second, remember that it's okay to be honest with God. If you are feeling frustrated, or even angry, at what God is doing (or not doing), let Him know. He isn't surprised, or disappointed, or angry about our feelings. When we express our frustrations to God, we are telling Him that we trust Him enough to take care of them. After all, if God weren't God, we wouldn't be angry when we think

He isn't working. Express yourself, and watch what He does to show you His essential goodness.

Third, remember that you need to start praising God before you start to see Him work. It may take time to understand what God is doing. But we need to show our faith and begin to praise Him before we see His work. We know that He is working. We know that all His plans are good. We know that He works everything out for our good. So the time to start praising Him is now. He will reveal His plan in time. Until then, praise Him!

We cannot think of anything better than the thought of knowing that God is on our side. He showed us that He loved us by sending Jesus to die for us. And He shows us again every day by the way He blesses us. Even in stressful times, He is worthy of our praise.

A FINAL WORD

Throughout this book, we have used Pastor Alex Average to illustrate the destructive aspects of stress — the way it negatively affects your life and ministry. We have also told stories of Pastor Rob Renegade, who has learned the skills necessary to manage stress effectively. Although the names are fictitious, the situations are all too real. We have seen far too many pastors taken out of ministry early because they could not deal with the stress.

We are not talking about weak people here. These were strong, bright, dedicated men and women of God who loved Jesus with everything they had. But the stress got to be too much for them and they had to do something else, for their sake and the good of their families. It's a heartbreaking reality that is being lived out all over the world right now.

Our prayer is that this book has given you some tools you can use to fight the effects of stress. We hope that because you read this book, your life and ministry will be a bit more joyful, a bit more relaxed, a bit more focused on what's important. If we have done that, we have done our job.

WHAT GOD WANTS YOUR MINISTRY TO BE

Our goal in this book, and my (Nelson's) goal in my years of coaching pastors all over the world, is to help you make your ministry into what God intends for it to be. We believe that God has a specific plan for the life of every Christian. And that is especially true of pastors. But we also believe He has two goals in mind that apply to every local church pastor.

First, God wants our ministry to be *faithful*. He wants us to be constantly pursuing Him and His purposes throughout our ministry. He obviously wants us to remain free of any moral corruption. But He also expects that we will be actively engaged in the tasks He has called us to do.

Stress can interfere with our faithfulness in several ways. Physically, it can cut short our ministry due to ill or failing health. It can also rob us of the energy we need to pursue Him. Stress can so tax us emotionally that we aren't able to pour ourselves into people the way we know we should.

We talked in an earlier chapter about the spiritual effects of stress. Stress can cause us to see God as small or distant, while making our problems look bigger than they are. This, of course, leads to us being overwhelmed by everything that is coming at us. Instead of having a big God — one who can handle anything — we try to get by with a small God who can't take on anything. And that will spell ministry disaster!

Second, God intends for our ministry to be *fruitful*. He wants to see souls saved. He wants to see lives transformed by the power of the gospel. And He wants us to lead His people in making disciples of all the nations. We firmly believe that God will hold us accountable for how well we led His people into the works He created them to do.

Stress can make us less fruitful in many ways. In the previous section we talked about how stress can shorten the length of our ministry. If our pastoral career is twenty years shorter due to stress, we obviously lose out on those twenty years of potential fruitfulness. But stress can make us less fruitful in other ways as well.

As we have said before, stress can be overwhelming, taking over our entire lives. When that happens, we can easily lose sight of what God wants us to do. We get pulled away from what's important, from the things God calls us to. We should always keep in mind the things that will make us both faithful and fruitful in ministry. And we can be both of those only when we have our stress level under control. It isn't enough to ignore stress and hope it goes away. It won't. It will get worse, until it becomes a real obstacle in your life, ministry, or family. (Or, most likely, in all three!) The only solution is to deal with the stress using the strategies we outlined here.

USE WHAT'S USEFUL

Don't feel as though you have to use every strategy we talked about in this book. It's likely that as you were reading, some of the strategies stuck out to you as being more useful than others. That's perfectly okay. Use some of the strategies now. Some of them you may find useful later. Others you may never use at all. And that's fine.

Ministry is stressful. But we don't want any Renegade Pastor to be so overwhelmed with stress that it impairs their ministry effectiveness. Our prayer for you is that God would make you both faithful and fruitful as you do this most important work. May you continue to serve our great, gracious God with energy, passion, and vision, and lead your church to reach its full redemptive potential!

POSTSCRIPT

We hope this book will become a conversation starter between us. We are continually developing resources and gathering ideas to help you abandon average and fully live the Renegade Pastor lifestyle. Let's stay in touch, either indirectly, through your subscription to my free newsletter, or directly, as you officially join the Renegade Pastors Network. Find out about both at this book's website:

www.RenegadeStressManagement.com

You can also use the website to connect with me personally. I would love to hear your story and to continue discussing ways in which we can grow together for God's glory.

Your partner in ministry,

Nelson Searcy
Lead Pastor, The Journey Church
Lead "Renegade Pastor,"
www.RenegadePastors.com

Richard Jarman
Lead Pastor, TouchPoint Church
Bell Gardens, CA
Member, Renegade Pastors Network

ACKNOWLEDGEMENTS

Nelson Searcy: Stress has been a constant companion in my life. I have had a relationship with stress since I was a young teenager writing computer programs under impossible deadlines. Entering ministry at age 18 and having now served the local church for almost 30 years, my relationship with stress has only intensified.

This book is the product of my attempt to manage, leverage, minimize and embrace this ever-present companion. The ideas in this book have helped me, my Journey Church staff (the church I pastor) and the hundreds of pastors I have coached to deal with this never-ending (and all too often harmful) challenge of stress. I pray that our gracious Lord will use this book to help you, too. Stress is always going to be part of ministry, but it can be managed, leveraged and used for God's glory.

This is my second book with my friend and respected colleague, Richard Jarman. He has been a committed, professional and encouraging co-author. He has taken my principles and expanded them, personalized them and strengthened them. As a pastor and member of my coaching network, he has also lived the principles in this book. Also, as a superb writer, his contribution to this book cannot be understated.

On the same note and perhaps to an even greater extent, this book would not be possible without the tireless effort and commitment of my Church Leader Insights colleague, Sandra Olivieri. This is no overstatement. While I provided the content for the book and Richard provided the written words, it was Sandra who shepherded this project from concept to copy editing to cover to final creation. On behalf of Richard and myself, thank you Sandra!

Connected to Sandra, I must thank the entire Church Leader Insights team, all current and previous members of my coaching networks who have helped me develop the concepts in this book, and the staff of The Journey Church, especially my executive staff who bear the intense daily stress of leading a healthy and growing church. Finally, I must thank my family for their ongoing support. Kelley and I will celebrate 24 years of marriage right around the release time of this book. My son, Alexander, will turn 12 going on 16. While Richard and Sandra made this book possible, my family makes everything I do a ministry of greater joy and significance through their support, prayer and partnership.

One final note: Like Richard, I battled health issues the entire writing of this book. Often outlining chapters from the chemo chair and then editing the final pages after a major surgery to remove colon cancer. The irony of writing a stress book while under the greatest stress of my life. Yet, with all sincerity, God was/is/will be faithful through it all. Amen.

Richard Jarman: This has been an interesting project for me. I have battled some health issues during the writing of this book, which has made completing it a challenge, to say the least. But through it all I have felt God's hand on what I've put into words. My prayer is that God uses these words to bless and strengthen pastors, a group of people I love with all I have.

I must first of all thank Jesus Christ for saving me, and putting me into pastoral ministry. I serve TouchPoint Church, the greatest church in the world. I am grateful that they gave me the time and space I needed to finish this project. I love each member of my TPC family. I appreciate your prayers, and I'm looking forward to many more years of turning our community upside down with you!

God called me to be a husband and father above all else, and I couldn't be happier about it. My kids are a constant source of joy and wonder. Samuel, Grace, Abigail, Joseph, and Hope: I see God at work in each of you. I can't wait to see what God has in store for you. And to my amazing, beautiful wife, Jennifer: I am blessed every day by your love and faithfulness. Thank you. I love you!

NOTES

INTRODUCTION

1. R. J. Krejcir Ph.D. "Continuing Research On Pastors" Francis A. Schaeffer Institute of Church Leadership Development. 2007 (research from 1989 to 2006).

2. Kaldor, Peter, and Rod Bullpitt. Burnout In Church Leaders. Openbook: Adelaide, 2001.

3. Stetzer, Ed. "Pastoral Ministry Makes Me Feel Lonely At Times." Lifeway Research phone survey. Taken August 17-24, 2011.

CHAPTER 5 – TAKE MINI-BREAKS

1. Hunter, Emily, PhD., and Cindy Wu, PhD. "Give Me a Better Break: Choosing Workday Break Activities to Maximize Resource Recovery." Baylor University Media Communications, September 9, 2015.

2. Haid, Michael. "Just One-in-Five Employees Take Actual Lunch Break." Right Management survey, taken September-October, 2012.

A Snapshot of the Renegade Way

The Seven Commitments
of a Renegade Pastor™

By Nelson Searcy

Commitment One: I WILL FOLLOW MY LORD

Am I valuing my relationship with God above all other relationships?

Matt. 6:33; Mark 8:34; Phil. 1:21-24

Commitment Two: I WILL LOVE MY FAMILY

Am I sacrificing my family on the altar of ministry?

Matt. 19:4-6; Eph. 5:25-33; Eph. 6:4

Commitment Three: I WILL FULFILL MY CALLING

Am I using my gifts and abilities to become all that God has called me to be?

1 Tim. 3:1-7; 1 Pet. 5:1-4

Commitment Four: I WILL MANAGE MY TIME

Am I in control of my most limited commodity?

Ps. 39:4-5; Eph. 5:15-17

Commitment Five: I WILL SHEPHERD MY FLOCK

Am I effectively leading, feeding and protecting the sheep under my care?

Acts 20:28; 1 Pet. 5:2-4

Commitment Six: I WILL MAXIMIZE MY CHURCH

Am I doing everything I can to lead my church for maximum impact?

Matt. 10:16; Acts 2:42-47; 1 Cor. 3:7-8

Commitment Seven: I WILL EXPAND GOD'S KINGDOM

Am I leading my church to reach its full redemptive potential?

Matt. 28:18-20; Luke 10:2; 2 Tim. 4:5

© Nelson Searcy

To learn more about being a Renegade Pastor, go to:
www.RenegadeStressManagement.com

ADDITIONAL BOOKS
BY NELSON SEARCY:

 Launch: Starting a New Church From Scratch
Topic: Church Planting

 The Healthy Renegade Pastor: Abandoning Average in Your Health and Wellness
Topics: Leadership, Health

 The Difference Maker: Using Your Everyday Life For Eternal Impact
Topics: Evangelism, Spiritual Growth

 The Renegade Pastor's Guide to Time Management
Topic: Leadership

 The Renegade Pastor: Abandoning Average in Your Life and Ministry
Topic: Leadership

 Ignite: How to Spark Immediate Growth in Your Church
Topics: Growth Barriers, Evangelism

 Maximize: How to Develop Extravagant Givers in Your Church
Topic: Stewardship

 The Generosity Ladder: Your Next Step to Financial Peace
Topic: Stewardship

 Connect: How to Double Your Number of Volunteers
Topic: Ministry

 The Greatness Principle: Finding Significance and Joy by Serving Others
Topic: Ministry

 Engage: A Guide to Creating Life-Transforming Worship Services
Topic: Worship Planning

 Revolve: A New Way to See Worship
Topic: Worship Planning

 Fusion: Turning First-Time Guests Into Fully-Engaged Members of Your Church
Topic: Assimilation

 Activate: An Entirely New Approach to Small Groups
Topic: Small Groups

These books are available at www.Amazon.com and www.ChristianBook.com
For other resources, visit our websites:

www.ChurchLeaderInsights.com
www.RenegadePastors.com

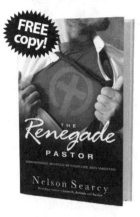

How HEALTHY is Your Church?

Get a FREE COPY of Nelson Searcy's Revised & Expanded *8 Systems of a Healthy Church* e-book! ($23.95 value)

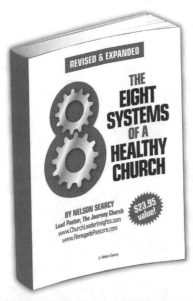

God designed all the parts of the body – both the church body and the physical body – to work together, allowing us to fulfill his purposes and plans on this earth. And both of those respective bodies function best through well-developed systems.

Nelson Searcy's revised & expanded *8 Systems of a Healthy Church* e-book has been updated with new chapters for Assimilation and Stewardship. Learn from pastors who have been using the systems in their own churches. Get practical help as you lead your church to greater health and effectiveness.

Download your FREE e-book now ($23.95 value):
www.ChurchLeaderInsights.com/systems